Safe DATES

An Adolescent Dating Abuse Prevention Curriculum

Second Edition

Vangie Foshee, Ph.D., and Stacey Langwick, Ph.D.

HAZELDEN®

Hazelden
Center City, Minnesota 55012
hazelden.org

ISBN: 978-1-59285-922-1

Cover design by David Spohn
Interior design by Kinne Design
Interior illustrations by Patrice Barton

"In my opinion, Safe Dates *is clearly the best available program. We will be taking a major step toward prevention of family violence if every teenager has the benefit of this program."*

— MURRAY A. STRAUS
Professor of Sociology and Co-Director Family Research
Laboratory, University of New Hampshire

"The prevention of dating abuse is an important step in reducing the larger problem of violence against women. Reducing dating abuse requires effective prevention tools that are scientifically based. Recognizing the lack of such tools, CDC funded the development of the Safe Dates *program. We hope that the lessons learned from the program can be used by other communities in their efforts to prevent violence."*

— DR. RODNEY HAMMOND, PH.D.
Director, Division of Violence Prevention, National Center for
Injury Prevention and Control, Centers for Disease Control
and Prevention

*"*Safe Dates *is the best evaluated program for changing attitudes and behavior. It is a program for general use for all students in a middle or high school, and follow-up data showed that the program had effects lasting four years."*

— K. DANIEL O'LEARY
Distinguished Professor of Psychology, Stony Brook University

"Domestic violence is a serious health and safety issue for our country, and it often starts in adolescence. All involved agree that prevention is one of the most important ways to address the problem. Safe Dates *is one of the only tested and supported prevention programs that can be used in schools for young adolescents. I recommend it highly, and I hope it will be used widely."*

— JACQUELYN C. CAMPBELL, PH.D., RN, FAAN
Domestic Violence Researcher and Policy Advocate
Author of *Assessing Dangerousness* and *Empowering Survivors of Abuse*

CONTENTS

Introductory Materials

How to Use the CD-ROM 1

Introduction to the Curriculum 3

Introduction to Teen Dating Abuse 16

Curriculum Scope and Sequence 24

Related National Academic Standards 26

Session Descriptions and Preparation 29

The Sessions

Session 1: Defining Caring Relationships 31

Session 2: Defining Dating Abuse 43

Session 3: Why Do People Abuse? 57

Session 4: How to Help Friends 71

Session 5: Helping Friends 83

Session 6: Overcoming Gender Stereotypes 93

Session 7: How We Feel, How We Deal 107

Session 8: Equal Power through Communication 119

Session 9: Preventing Dating Sexual Abuse 131

Session 10: Reviewing the *Safe Dates* Program 145

How to Use the CD-ROM

This manual comes with a CD-ROM that contains downloadable and printable resources, including all the student handouts and parent materials needed for implementing *Safe Dates*. All of the resources are in PDF format and can be accessed using Adobe Reader. If you do not have Adobe Reader, you can download it for free at www.adobe.com.

Whenever you see this icon ▯ in the manual, this means the resource needed is located on the CD-ROM. An SP symbol (SP) near the icon indicates that a Spanish version of the document is also available on the CD-ROM. All of the parent materials for *Safe Dates* have been translated into Spanish.

To access the resources on the CD-ROM, put the disc in your computer's CD-ROM player. Open your version of Adobe Reader, and then open the documents by clicking on the ones you wish to use. These resources cannot be modified, but they can be printed for use without concern for copyright infringement.

Introduction to the Curriculum

What Is *Safe Dates?*

The *Safe Dates* program is a dating abuse prevention program consisting of five components:

1. a ten-session dating abuse curriculum

2. a play about dating abuse

3. a poster contest

4. parent materials, including a letter, newsletter, and the Families for Safe Dates program

5. an evaluation questionnaire

All the materials needed to implement the program are included in this manual and CD-ROM. The following is a brief description of each component of the *Safe Dates* program.

Ten-Session Curriculum

The *Safe Dates* curriculum is a ten-session program that deals with attitudes and behaviors associated with dating abuse and violence. Each session can be completed in about fifty minutes. The curriculum can be presented over a period of days or weeks, depending on your program's schedule.

Each session includes detailed instructions on presenting the information, activities to reinforce the key concepts, and reproducible student handouts. Within the session outlines, all text that is **bold** is scripted text. While leading the sessions, facilitators may choose to read this text from the manual, use it as a guide, or not use it at all.

Most of the sessions provide tips for altering the activities to shorten the time required to complete the sessions. If you don't have enough time to present all ten sessions, consider using the following six-session or four-session program:

- *Six-Session Program:* Combine sessions 1 and 2; do all the activities in session 3; combine sessions 4 and 5; do all the activities in session 6; combine sessions 7 and 8; and do all the activities in session 9.

- *Four-Session Program:* Combine sessions 1 and 2; do all the activities in session 3; combine sessions 4 and 5; and do all the activities in session 9.

It is important to realize, however, that the fidelity of the product and the accompanying outcomes are best maintained by completing all ten sessions.

This program also includes an optional exam that can be given to students prior to beginning *Safe Dates* and/or after the program is completed to assess knowledge gained by the students. This exam is located on the CD-ROM.

Dating Abuse Play

Before implementing the *Safe Dates* curriculum, plan to stage *There's No Excuse for Dating Abuse,* a forty-five-minute play about dating abuse and violence, which was written by high school drama students. Before presenting the play, consider sharing local statistics on the prevalence of teen dating abuse. Following the performance, have the actors lead discussions, preferably in small groups, with the audience about the issues presented in the play.

Consider presenting this play during a schoolwide assembly, as part of your school's drama program, or at other school or community events. You don't need professional actors. Enlist the help of your school's drama department or have your own students perform the play.

When preparing students/actors for the play, familiarize them with the *Safe Dates* curriculum, provide them with local

As part of your *Safe Dates* program, plan to stage a forty-five-minute play about dating abuse and violence.

domestic abuse prevention resources, and/or introduce them to professionals in the field. The script for the play is located on the CD-ROM.

Poster Contest

Hosting a poster contest is a great way to reinforce the concepts learned in this curriculum. Instructions for the poster contest are included in session 10 (see pages 148–149). Posters about dating abuse prevention can be displayed in school hallways or other community buildings such as libraries, city hall, or shopping malls.

Students could also use their posters in presentations to various school or community groups. Have students vote on their favorite poster. Consider giving a cash prize or nice gift to the winners of first, second, and third place.

Parent Materials

As in every strong prevention effort, it is important to get your students' parents or guardians involved in your *Safe Dates* program. A letter informing caregivers of the *Safe Dates* program is located on the CD-ROM, as is a two-page education newsletter that you can send to parents and guardians or keep on hand, in case you need to talk to a caregiver about this issue. Consider mailing the letter and newsletter together.

For those teachers and families who choose to dig deeper into the issue of adolescent dating abuse, Families for Safe Dates is a comprehensive, research-based program included on the CD-ROM. Families for Safe Dates includes six booklets that contain background information and activities for caregivers and teens to do together as they learn about different topics regarding adolescent dating abuse.

More detailed information on how to deliver the Families for Safe Dates program is described in the Introduction to Families for Safe Dates file on the CD-ROM.

Evaluating Safe Dates in Your School

Many organizations and schools using *Safe Dates* have expressed a desire to perform a formal evaluation of the program. Thus, included on the CD-ROM of this second edition of *Safe Dates* is the *Safe Dates* Evaluation Questionnaire that can be used to do a formal evaluation of the *Safe Dates* program if desired.

The *Safe Dates* Evaluation Questionnaire assesses the knowledge, attitudes, skills, and behaviors that *Safe Dates* is designed to change. This questionnaire will be most valuable when it is administered both to students taking *Safe Dates* and to students not taking *Safe Dates,* for comparison. An ideal evaluation design is one where students, classrooms, or schools are randomly selected to receive *Safe Dates*. Because of confidentiality issues, student names should not be included on this questionnaire. Choose staff members who are not implementing *Safe Dates* in the classroom to administer and analyze the results from this questionnaire. Make sure they follow all the procedures required by your local human subjects review board. It is recommended that the questionnaire be administered after the students have been exposed to the play, the curriculum, and the poster contest.

A more informal evaluation can be accomplished using the exam mentioned on page 4 as a pre-test and post-test, or just as a post-test to assess knowledge gained.

> The *Safe Dates* Evaluation Questionnaire can be used to do a formal evaluation of the *Safe Dates* program if desired.

What Are the Goals of the *Safe Dates* Program?

This program strives to

- raise students' awareness of what constitutes healthy and abusive dating relationships
- raise students' awareness of dating abuse and its causes and consequences
- equip students with the skills and resources to help themselves or friends in abusive dating relationships

> This program strives to raise students' awareness of what constitutes healthy and abusive dating relationships.

- equip students with the skills to develop healthy dating relationships, including positive communication, anger management, and conflict resolution

For more information on the learner outcomes for each session, turn to the curriculum's Scope and Sequence on pages 24 and 25.

Who Is the Intended Audience?

Safe Dates can be used as a dating abuse prevention tool for middle and high school students, both male and female. *Safe Dates* would fit well within a health education, family life, or general life skills curriculum (see the reference to national academic standards on page 26).

Because dating abuse is often tied to the abuse of alcohol and other drugs, you may want to consider using *Safe Dates* in conjunction with drug and alcohol prevention programs, as well as any other general violence prevention programs. For example, *Safe Dates* would work well with Hazelden's high school *Class Action* curriculum when discussing the issue of alcohol and date rape.

Some schools have trained student peer leaders who could teach or assist in teaching the *Safe Dates* program. If you use peer leaders, try to select or have peers select teens whom students respect and admire. You may also want to consider having older teens teach younger teens.

A school counselor could offer *Safe Dates* as part of a support group or counseling/education program, or it could be used in afterschool, community youth enrichment (such as YMCA or Girl Scouts), and faith-based youth programs.

Safe Dates could also be used as an intervention tool at domestic abuse or crisis centers, in juvenile diversion programs, and with victim support groups.

▼
Safe Dates can be used as a dating abuse prevention tool for middle and high school students, both male and female.

▼
Safe Dates could also be used as an intervention tool at domestic abuse or crisis centers and with victim support groups.

Duplicating this page is illegal. Do not copy this material without written permission from the publisher.

7

Is *Safe Dates* a Research-based Program?

Safe Dates is a research-based program with strong, long-term outcomes. It has been identified as a model program in the National Registry of Evidence-based Programs and Practices (NREPP) as well as many other federal- and foundation-funded publications.

Safe Dates was the subject of substantial formative research in fourteen public schools in North Carolina using a rigorous experimental design. The program was found to be effective in both preventing dating abuse perpetration and victimization and in reducing perpetration and victimization among teens already involved in dating abuse. Adolescents participating in the program, as compared with those who did not, also reported less acceptance of dating abuse, less of a tendency to gender stereotype, and a greater awareness of community services for dating abuse.

Researchers studied the same group of students four years after implementation and found that students who participated in the *Safe Dates* program reported 56 percent to 92 percent less physical, serious physical, and sexual dating violence victimization and perpetration than teens who didn't participate in *Safe Dates*. The program has been found to be equally effective for males and females and for minority and non-minority adolescents.

For more information on the research behind *Safe Dates*, consult the following journal articles:

– Foshee, Vangie A., Fletcher Linder, Karl Bauman, Stacey Langwick, Ximena Arriaga, Janet Heath, Pam McMahon, and Shrikant Bangdiwala. "The Safe Dates Project: Theoretical Basis, Evaluation Design, and Selected Baseline Findings." *American Journal of Preventive Medicine (supplement)* 12, no. 5 (1996).

– Foshee, Vangie A., Karl Bauman, Ximena Arriaga, Russ Helms, Gary Koch, and Fletcher Linder. "An Evaluation of Safe Dates, an Adolescent Dating Violence Prevention Program." *American Journal of Public Health* 88, no. 1 (January 1998).

▼

Safe Dates is a research-based program with strong, long-term outcomes.

– Foshee, Vangie A., Karl E. Bauman, Susan Ennett, Chirayath Suchindran, Thad Benefield, and Fletcher Linder. "Assessing the Effects of the Dating Violence Prevention Program *Safe Dates* Using Random Coefficient Regression Modeling." *Prevention Science* 6, no. 3 (2005).

– Foshee, Vangie A., Karl Bauman, Susan Ennett, Fletcher Linder, Thad Benefield, and Chirayath Suchindran. "Assessing the Long-term Effects of the Safe Dates Program and a Booster in Preventing and Reducing Adolescent Dating Violence Victimization and Perpetration." *American Journal of Public Health* 94, no. 4 (2004).

How Is *Safe Dates* Different from Other Dating Abuse Programs?

Besides being strongly research-based, *Safe Dates* is unique in several ways:

1. It can be used as both a prevention and an intervention tool.

2. It considers both boys and girls as potential abusive partners and victims of dating abuse.

3. It includes activities that address both the victim and the abusive partner.

4. It is designed for general populations of adolescents rather than only those at high risk.

5. It is structured to reach large numbers of adolescents.

6. It is theoretically based.

Safe Dates considers both boys and girls as potential abusive partners and victims of dating abuse.

What Is the Theoretical Base of *Safe Dates*?

The theoretical base for the *Safe Dates* primary prevention activities includes promoting changes in norms tied with improvements in conflict management skills. Adolescents develop behavioral norms by observing acceptable behaviors, consequences, or reactions of those close to them. Peers are a primary source of influence for adolescents. Many studies have found that adolescents see few negative consequences from their peers for dating abuse. This perceived acceptance of dating abuse, which may indicate the norms associated with dating abuse, is one of the strongest causes of dating abuse. Therefore, *Safe Dates* includes many activities designed to alter the perceived norms of dating abuse by increasing adolescents' perceptions of the negative consequences of dating abuse and changing peer responses to dating abuse.

As another indicator of dating abuse acceptance, cognitive-development theories suggest that adolescents form norms related to how males and females should act, and then strive to become like those categories they have created. In fact, gender stereotyping is stronger during adolescence than at any other time. Many studies have found that norms related to gender roles are associated with partner abuse. Thus, *Safe Dates* also includes many activities to change norms related to gender roles and stereotypes.

Safe Dates also includes two full sessions that teach conflict management techniques, because violent couples report using flawed conflict management and negotiation techniques that leave a conflict unresolved, which can lead to the use of physical and psychological abuse.

Changes in dating abuse, gender-role norms, and conflict management skills are also important for secondary prevention (such as encouraging victims to leave abusive partners and perpetrators to stop abusing their partners). In addition, the *Safe Dates* secondary prevention activities are guided by principles of Weinstein's Precaution Adoption Theory. This theory suggests that before someone will take a preventive action (such as leaving an abusive partner, seeking help for dating abuse, or stopping the perpetration of dating abuse), the person needs to believe that he or she needs help and that the efforts for getting help will be successful. As a result, *Safe Dates* includes activities designed to increase victims' and perpetrators' beliefs that they need help and to increase their awareness of community services from which they could seek help.

> *Safe Dates* includes many activities designed to alter the perceived norms of dating abuse.

> *Safe Dates* also includes many activities to change norms related to gender roles and stereotypes.

How Can I Address Dating Abuse on a Schoolwide Level?

Whenever possible, *Safe Dates* should be taught within a school or organizational environment that supports healthy dating relationships and doesn't tolerate dating abuse. Sometimes adults downplay the seriousness of teen dating abuse. The truth is, teen relationships can become as abusive and violent as adult relationships.

Here are some ways schools and community organizations can promote and support the message that dating abuse is not tolerated:

1. Set clear school policies about reporting dating abuse or violence of any kind, whether it occurs on campus or not.

2. Work to create a school environment where respect and responsibility are promoted and violence and sexual harassment are not.

3. If a student has obtained a restraining order or other court order due to dating abuse, take the situation seriously and proactively enforce the order on campus.

4. Train staff to recognize the signs of dating abuse and to intervene appropriately.

5. Teach the *Safe Dates* program to all students. Make program participation mandatory.

6. Perform the *There's No Excuse for Dating Abuse* play for all students and possibly parents and other community members.

7. Host a schoolwide dating abuse prevention campaign. Involve students in making posters, announcements, and other promotional events on this important issue.

8. Make young people aware of dating abuse prevention resources at school or in the community. Invite community representatives to speak to students about this issue.

9. Involve parents by hosting a parent education program, such as the evidence-based Families for Safe Dates program (included on the CD-ROM), sending home the

> Whenever possible, *Safe Dates* should be taught within a school or organizational environment that supports healthy dating relationships and doesn't tolerate dating abuse.

parent education newsletter (included on the CD-ROM), or talking directly with parents of students you suspect are either victims of dating abuse or abusive partners.

10. Offer school events that promote group activities rather than individual dating (such as community service projects and class parties).

What Resources Are Available in My Community to Help with This Topic?

You don't need to be an expert on dating abuse to teach *Safe Dates*. However, you may want to turn to community resources for help in presenting this issue or to learn more about it.

Most communities have a domestic abuse crisis center or hotline. Check your local phone book or call the National Teen Dating Abuse Helpline at 1-866-331-9474 or the National Domestic Violence Hotline at 1-800-799-SAFE (7233). These services will provide emergency and nonemergency referrals to teen dating abuse and domestic violence resources in your area. Also check with your county's mental health service agency or local university.

Most crisis centers offer brochures or other informational materials you can hand out to students. They may also have staff who can teach or team-teach the curriculum or provide you with local statistics (to be used in session 2).

If I Work for a Domestic Violence Prevention Program, Could I Provide *Safe Dates* in My Area Schools?

Often domestic violence crisis centers or community programs are looking for ways to partner with area schools on the issue of dating abuse prevention. *Safe Dates* may provide an avenue for this partnership.

Schools may be seeking community professionals to train teachers in using the *Safe Dates* program or to directly teach the curriculum to students. In some cases, schools may even be willing to pay a stipend for this expertise.

> You don't need to be an expert on dating abuse to teach *Safe Dates*.

What Are Some Things I Should Be Aware of in Teaching *Safe Dates*?

Here are some helpful tips on teaching the *Safe Dates* program:

1. During the first session, it's important to create a sense of trust and safety in your group. Be sure to discuss the need for ground rules (as outlined in session 1). Make sure students abide by these rules throughout the program.

2. Make sure students do not use real names or too many details when talking about other people.

3. Be aware that some students in your class may be experiencing dating abuse or other abuse, perhaps at home. Don't force students to answer questions if they're uncomfortable doing so.

4. It's difficult in a class environment to guarantee complete confidentiality. Warn students of this fact, so they don't reveal too much.

5. Maintain respect during discussions. Allow people to offer opposing views, but do so respectfully.

6. When doing role-plays, do not allow students to act out abusive or violent behavior. The role-plays in the curriculum are written to prevent this, but you should guard against this as well.

7. When talking about sexual issues, be respectful of all students. Some students will feel comfortable talking about sexual violence, and others may not. Use discretion in how you approach this subject in session 9.

8. Be aware of the important role that culture plays in addressing dating abuse. Some students may come from cultural backgrounds that make it more difficult to address this issue (for example, in some cultures dating is frowned upon; if a student is dating secretly, it may be hard to seek help for abuse).

> During the first session, it's important to create a sense of trust and safety in your group.

Other Guidelines as You Teach *Safe Dates*

1. **What if a student reveals she or he or a friend is a victim of dating abuse or other type of abuse or is an abusive partner?**

   While you're teaching *Safe Dates,* a student may reveal that he or she is either a victim of dating abuse or some other abuse or an abusive partner. It's important at the outset of the program to let students know what you'll do upon learning this information, so they don't feel set up or betrayed by the action you take.

   Before teaching *Safe Dates,* check whether your school has a policy on reporting abuse of any kind. Also contact your local domestic violence crisis center or county officials for guidance.

   If a student reveals information during a class discussion, do not continue discussing the issue with everyone present. Invite the student to talk privately with you afterward. Write down any information the student provides.

   Don't try to solve the problem on your own. Consult with appropriate school officials and the student's parents or guardians.

   Also use these steps (as outlined in session 4) when someone reveals dating abuse:

   a. Don't gossip.

   b. Believe the story.

   c. Tell the person that he or she didn't deserve to be abused.

   d. Let the person make his or her own decisions.

   e. Make a safety plan.

   f. Give help.

▼

If a student reveals personal information about dating abuse during a class discussion, do not continue discussing the issue with everyone present.

2. What if you believe a student is in imminent physical danger?

A student may reveal that she or he is in imminent danger of being harmed by a dating partner. Take these confessions seriously. Take action to help the student by talking with the appropriate school officials, as well as the student's parents and law officials.

3. What if parents are uncomfortable with the topic and don't want their children involved?

On rare occasions, parents may express reservations about the *Safe Dates* program. Sometimes, this is because they're unfamiliar with its content. Allow parents to review the curriculum. *Safe Dates* doesn't contain any sexually explicit information and it doesn't promote or push dating. Some parents may not want their children dating until an older age. Be sure to respect and support their decision.

Tell parents about the prevalence of dating abuse among teens and the importance of addressing the issue in a preventative way. Discuss any additional concerns they may have. If parents still voice reservations, it may be best to have the students complete an alternative project on a related topic.

▼

Safe Dates doesn't contain any sexually explicit information and it doesn't promote or push dating.

Introduction to Teen Dating Abuse

Why is it important to teach students so early—even in middle school—about dating abuse and its prevention?

JENNIFER'S STORY*

Jennifer met Tony in the eighth grade. They started dating shortly after they met and were soon inseparable. As time went on, Tony became more and more possessive of Jennifer. He would meet her after each class, so she couldn't spend time with her friends. Jennifer thought this was just Tony's way of showing how much he loved her.

Tony's possessiveness and jealousy continued to grow. He accused Jennifer of flirting with other guys. One day, he even hit her. Jennifer was confused. Was this the same Tony she had fallen in love with? The next day Tony showed up with flowers, asking for forgiveness.

The relationship became more abusive over time. Eventually, Jennifer tried to break up with Tony, but he threatened to harm her and himself if she did. Jennifer's parents got a restraining order against Tony, but it was very difficult to follow through on. After all, Jennifer and Tony were only teens; they weren't married or living together.

Even with a restraining order, Tony followed Jennifer around at school because school officials didn't try to enforce the order. After all, dating abuse isn't a big issue for teens, or so school officials thought.

The story tragically ended one day when Tony attacked Jennifer after school with a knife, stabbing her to death. Everyone wondered what had gone wrong, why they hadn't seen how serious the situation was. But how could they have known? After all, Tony and Jennifer were only teens. 🌀

---

* *This story is loosely based on a true story of a young woman who died due to dating violence.*

All kinds of people suffer from abuse in dating relationships: girls and boys; whites, African Americans, Native Americans, Hispanics, and Asians; students born in rich neighborhoods and students born in poor neighborhoods; people who come from abusive homes and people who do not; people who have dated a lot and people who have just begun dating. Children as young as twelve years old can be in abusive dating relationships.

Dating abuse is a very real issue for many students:

- In the United States, approximately 12 percent of heterosexual high school boys and girls report having been physically victimized by a dating partner in the previous year. This percentage is as high as 40 percent in some areas of the country.[1]

- Approximately 13 percent of gay adolescent girls and 9 percent of gay adolescent boys report having been physically victimized by a dating partner in the previous year.[2]

- Victimization from psychological dating abuse is even higher, with approximately 29 percent of heterosexual high school students and 20 percent of gay high school students reporting having been psychologically abused by a date in the previous year.[3]

- Dating abuse is beginning as early as the sixth grade.[4]

- Adults who use violence with their dating partners often begin doing so during adolescence, with the first episode typically occurring by age fifteen.[5]

- Young women between the ages of fourteen and seventeen represent 38 percent of those victimized by date rape.[6]

- Rapes by acquaintances account for 60 percent of all rapes reported to rape crisis centers.[7]

- Both girls and boys are victims of dating abuse, though girls receive more severe injuries from dating abuse than boys.[8]

- Both girls and boys are perpetrators of dating abuse, though girls tend to use less severe forms of dating abuse than boys.[9]

▼

Adults who use violence with their dating partners often begin doing so during adolescence.

- Abuse almost always recurs in a relationship. It doesn't just go away.

- Most abuse gets more severe over time.

- The consequences of being a victim of dating abuse for both boys and girls include depression, cigarette smoking, and suicide attempts. Additional consequences for girls are marijuana use, illicit substance use, and antisocial behavior; an additional consequence for boys is suicide ideation.[10]

What Is Dating Abuse?

Dating abuse includes any behavior by a dating partner that

- is used to *manipulate*

- is used to *gain control*

- is used to *gain power over* someone

- makes a person *feel bad* about himself or herself or other people who are close to this person (such as friends or family)

- makes a person *afraid* of her or his boyfriend or girlfriend

Abusive behaviors may include the following.

PHYSICALLY ABUSIVE:

– hitting	– pushing
– pinching	– using a weapon
– shaking	– biting
– throwing things	– threatening
– scratching	– spitting
– choking	– pulling hair
– shoving	

PSYCHOLOGICALLY/EMOTIONALLY ABUSIVE:

- ignoring a date's feelings

- insulting a date's beliefs or values

PSYCHOLOGICALLY/EMOTIONALLY ABUSIVE *continued:*

- acting in an intimidating way
- using sexually derogatory names
- calling a date names
- isolating a date from others
- driving recklessly to scare a date
- displaying inappropriate anger
- damaging personal property
- scaring a date
- keeping a date from leaving
- putting down family and friends
- humiliating a date in public or private
- telling lies
- purposefully injuring an animal
- threatening to hurt oneself

SEXUALLY ABUSIVE:

- forcing a date to have sex
- forcing a date to do other sexual things he or she doesn't want to do

It's important to realize that an abusive boyfriend or girl-friend can use physical or emotional attacks and that emotional abuse can be as serious as physical abuse.

Adolescents also use cell phones, e-mail, instant messaging (IM), text messages, Web chats, blogs, and social networking sites such as MySpace or Facebook to abuse dating partners. These technologies are being used to send insults, show private and embarrassing pictures of dating partners to others, monitor the activities of dating partners, spread rumors about dating partners, and frighten and threaten dating partners.

Why Is Dating Abuse Such a Prevalent Issue with Teens?

Teens May Not Take the Issue Seriously

The prevalence of dating abuse among teens may be partly attributed to their view of it. Teen victims tend to minimize the seriousness of the situation. Many of them see abuse as a "normal" part of relationships. Romanticizing about love, teens may interpret jealousy, possessiveness, and abuse as signs of love. *Safe Dates* addresses this issue in sessions 1 and 2 by defining what is a "normal," healthy relationship and what is abuse.

> Teen victims tend to minimize the seriousness of the situation.

Teens may also experience a lot of pressure to be in dating relationships. Consequently, a teen may remain in an abusive relationship just to have someone to date. The fear of not being liked may also prompt a teen to comply with an abusive partner's requests.

In addition, teens' communication skills are less developed than those of adults, and gender stereotyping, which has been associated with dating abuse, is stronger during adolescence than at any other time in life.

Adults May Not Take the Issue Seriously

Adults also confound the problem, as they often fail to take teen dating abuse seriously, believing teens will just grow out of it. However, teen dating abuse can be as violent as that of adults, and rather than growing out of the violence, teens are more likely to grow into it—establishing lifelong abuse patterns.

> Adults often fail to take teen dating abuse seriously, believing teens will just grow out of it.

Also, many young people are reluctant to talk to adults. Although this is a normal part of adolescence, such hesitation can prevent them from seeking help for abuse. Teens in abusive relationships will often confide in a friend first. This is why *Safe Dates* spends two sessions (sessions 4 and 5) talking about how friends can be helpful.

Due to this teen reluctance, it's important that adults be proactive rather than wait for teens to ask for help. If an adult suspects dating abuse, she or he should address the issue right away.

The Legal System May Not Help Either

Adolescents struggling with dating abuse sometimes face obstacles in the legal system. Many domestic violence laws do not include dating abuse in their definition, and in many courts, minors do not have a legal presence. Minors sometimes cannot file a civil case or ask for a restraining order unless a guardian appears with them in court. However, these obstacles are rapidly decreasing as more and more courts are becoming aware of the importance of protecting teens from dating abuse. Check with your court system to find out the local laws in your area related to protecting teens from dating abuse.

What Can We Do to Prevent Dating Abuse?

If abuse occurs once in a relationship, it's likely to occur again. Both men and women identify jealousy and uncontrollable anger as the main reasons for dating abuse. Abuse and violence are often used to establish power and control in a relationship. Any challenge to this power is seen as a threat.

The *Safe Dates* curriculum looks at why people abuse (session 3) and then identifies the key ways of preventing dating abuse, including changing gender stereotypes (session 6); dealing with feelings, particularly anger, in healthy, nonviolent ways (session 7); and promoting healthy communication and equal power in relationships (session 8).

Session 9 addresses the serious issue of dating sexual abuse and date rape. *Safe Dates* teaches teens how to protect themselves from dating sexual abuse, while stressing that the victim is never to blame.

Dating abuse is a serious issue that should be taken up with students as early as possible. Showing students how to develop positive, healthy dating relationships will help prevent dating abuse, not only when they're teens but in their future adult relationships as well.

> If abuse occurs once in a relationship, it's likely to occur again.

Notes

1. Centers for Disease Control and Prevention, "Youth Risk Behavior Surveillance—United States, 2007," *Surveillance Summaries, MMWR 2008;* 57 (No. SS-4). V. A. Foshee and R. Matthew, "Adolescent Dating Abuse Perpetration: A Review of Findings, Methodological Limitations, and Suggestions for Future Research," in *The Cambridge Handbook of Violent Behavior and Aggression,* ed. Daniel Flannery, Alexander Vazsonyi, and I. Waldman (New York: Cambridge University Press, 2007).

2. C. T. Halpern, M. L. Young, M. W. Waller, S. L. Martin, and L. L. Kupper, "Prevalence of Partner Violence in Same-Sex Romantic and Sexual Relationships in a National Sample of Adolescents," *Journal of Adolescent Health* 35, no. 2 (2004): 124–31.

3. Halpern et al., "Prevalence of Partner Violence." Carolyn Tucker Halpern, Selene G. Oslak, Mary L. Young, Sandra L. Martin, and Lawrence L. Kupper, "Partner Violence among Adolescents in Opposite-Sex Romantic Relationships: Findings from the National Longitudinal Study of Adolescent Health," *American Journal of Public Health* 91, no. 10 (October 2001).

4. S. Miller-Johnson, D. Gorman-Smith, T. Sullivan, P. Orpinas, T. R. Simon, "Parent and Peer Predictors of Physical Dating Violence Perpetration in Early Adolescence: Tests of Moderation and Gender Differences," *Journal of Clinical Child and Adolescent Psychology* 38, no. 4 (2009): 538–50. B. Taylor, N. Stein, A. R. Mack, T. J. Horwood, and F. Burden, *Experimental Evaluation of Gender Violence/Harassment Prevention Programs in Middle Schools. Final Report.* (National Institute of Justice, 2008).

5. J. Henton, R. Cate, J. Koval, S. Lloyd, and S. Christopher, "Romance and Violence in Dating Relationships," *Journal of Family Issues* 4, no. 3 (1983): 467–82.

6. Robin Warshaw, *I Never Called It Rape: The Ms. Report on Recognizing, Fighting and Surviving Date and Acquaintance Rape* (New York: Harper and Row, 1988).

7. Carol Sousa, "The Dating Violence Intervention Project," in *Dating Violence: Young Women in Danger,* ed. Barrie Levy (Englewood, NJ: Seal Press, 1998).

8. J. Archer, "Sex Differences in Aggression between Heterosexual Partners: A Meta-analytic Review," *Psychological Bulletin* 126 (2000): 651–80.

9. Archer, "Sex Differences." V. A. Foshee, T. Benefield, C. Suchindran, S. T. Ennett, K. E. Bauman, K. J. Karriker-Jaffe, H. L. McNaughton, and Reyes J. Mathias, "The Development of Four Types of Adolescent Dating Abuse and Selected Demographic Correlates," *Journal of Research on Adolescence* 19, no. 3 (2009): 380–400.

10. A. Brown, E. Cosgrave, E. Killackey, R. Purcell, J. Buckby, and A. Yung, "The Longitudinal Association of Adolescent Dating Violence with Psychiatric Disorders and Functioning," *Journal of Interpersonal Violence* (2008), DOI:10.1177/0886260508327700. D. M. Ackard, M. E. Eisenberg, and D. Neumark-Sztainer, "Long-term Impact of Adolescent Dating Violence on the Behavioral and Psychological Health of Male and Female Youth," *Journal of Pediatrics* 151 (2007): 476–81. T. A. Roberts, J. D. Klein, and S. Fisher, "Longitudinal Effect of Intimate Partner Abuse on High-Risk Behavior among Adolescents," *Archives of Pediatric Adolescent Medicine* 157 (2003): 875–81.

Curriculum Scope and Sequence

SESSION 1: **DEFINING CARING RELATIONSHIPS**	SESSION 2: **DEFINING DATING ABUSE**	SESSION 3: **WHY DO PEOPLE ABUSE?**	SESSION 4: **HOW TO HELP FRIENDS**	SESSION 5: **HELPING FRIENDS**
By the end of this session, students will be able to do the following:				
• identify the qualities that are most important to them in a dating relationship • identify actions that are caring and supportive • describe how they want to be treated by a dating partner • describe how they want to treat a dating partner • understand that they can and should choose how they'll be treated in a dating relationship • understand that they can and should choose how they'll treat a dating partner	• identify harmful dating behaviors • define physically and emotionally abusive behaviors • identify physical and emotional abuse in dating relationships • be more likely to identify abusive behaviors as abusive • be more aware of their susceptibility to dating abuse • be more likely to reject abuse as normal in dating relationships	• describe the controlling and manipulative functions of dating abuse • identify abusive behaviors as abusive • choose not to believe common misperceptions of why dating abuse happens • understand that dating abuse is a serious matter • understand that abuse is not the victim's fault • describe the serious short- and long-term consequences of abusive relationships • identify the warning signs that a person is a victim of abuse or is an abusive partner	• recognize the complexity of the decision to leave an abusive relationship and the many different opinions about when one should leave • recognize the difficulty and fear that a friend in an abusive relationship may have in reaching out for help • describe a variety of ways to support a friend who is a victim of dating abuse • describe the community resources available for teens in abusive dating relationships • seek help if they're victims of abuse or are abusive partners in a dating relationship	• identify red flags that indicate their friend might be an abusive partner or a victim of dating abuse • feel more comfortable confronting a friend who is abusive in a dating relationship • understand how to support a friend in an abusive relationship

SESSION 6: OVERCOMING GENDER STEREOTYPES	SESSION 7: HOW WE FEEL, HOW WE DEAL	SESSION 8: EQUAL POWER THROUGH COMMUNICATION	SESSION 9: PREVENTING DATING SEXUAL ABUSE	SESSION 10: REVIEWING THE *SAFE DATES* PROGRAM
By the end of this session, students will be able to do the following:				
• understand that they and other people hold specific images of dating relationships • describe how the images people hold influence their interactions in a dating relationship • identify the harmful consequences of gender stereotyping • explain the role that gender stereotyping plays in dating relationships	• express their feelings or emotions in various ways • understand the importance of acknowledging and communicating their feelings • identify situations that trigger their anger • identify physiological and psychological cues that they're angry • identify a variety of nonviolent ways to respond to anger • understand that they have a choice in how to respond to anger • increasingly use nonviolent responses to anger	• describe the four SAFE communication skills for resolving conflict • demonstrate the use of the four SAFE communication skills • describe some nonviolent responses when a dating partner doesn't communicate in a way that is fair and equal	• understand that victims of dating sexual abuse are never to blame • understand that rape is always unacceptable • understand and interpret "no" cues correctly • know how to protect themselves in a potential rape situation • state their sexual boundaries clearly to their dating partner • describe dating tips to decrease their chances of being a victim of sexual assault or an abusive partner • identify date rape drugs	• retain what they learned while participating in *Safe Dates*

Related National Academic Standards**

Using *Safe Dates* will help you meet the following national academic standards:

Health Education Standards (Sixth–Eighth Grade)

- Describe the influence of culture on health beliefs, practices, and behaviors.
- Describe how peers influence healthy and unhealthy behaviors.
- Analyze how messages from media influence health behaviors.
- Analyze the influence of technology on personal and family health.
- Explain how the perceptions of norms influence healthy and unhealthy behaviors.
- Access valid health information from home, school, and community.
- Describe situations that may require professional health services.
- Apply effective verbal and nonverbal communication skills to enhance health.
- Demonstrate refusal and negotiation skills that avoid or reduce health risks.
- Demonstrate effective conflict management or resolution strategies.
- Demonstrate how to ask for assistance to enhance the health of self and others.
- Identify circumstances that can help or hinder healthy decision making.

** Standards are taken from The Joint Committee on National Health Education Standards. *National Health Education Standards: Achieving Excellence* (2nd edition). Atlanta: The American Cancer Society, 2007.

- Explain the importance of assuming responsibility for personal health behaviors.

- Demonstrate healthy practices and behaviors that will maintain or improve the health of self and others.

- Demonstrate behaviors that avoid or reduce health risks to self and others.

- State a health-enhancing position on a topic and support it with accurate information.

- Demonstrate how to influence and support others to make positive health choices.

- Identify ways that health messages and communication techniques can be altered for different audiences.

Health Education Standards (Ninth–Twelfth Grade)

- Analyze how the culture supports and challenges health beliefs, practices, and behaviors.

- Analyze how peers influence healthy and unhealthy behaviors.

- Evaluate the effect of media on personal and family health.

- Evaluate the impact of technology on personal, family, and community health.

- Analyze how the perceptions of norms influence healthy and unhealthy behaviors.

- Use resources from home, school, and community that provide valid health information.

- Determine when professional health services may be required.

- Use skills for communicating effectively with family, peers, and others to enhance health.

- Demonstrate refusal, negotiation, and collaboration skills to enhance health and avoid or reduce health risks.

- Demonstrate strategies to prevent, manage, or resolve interpersonal conflicts without harming self or others.

- Demonstrate how to ask for and offer assistance to enhance the health of self and others.

- Examine barriers that can hinder healthy decision making.

- Analyze the role of individual responsibility for enhancing health.

- Demonstrate a variety of healthy practices and behaviors that will maintain or improve the health of self and others.

- Demonstrate a variety of behaviors that avoid or reduce health risks to self and others.

- Use accurate peer and societal norms to formulate a health-enhancing message.

- Demonstrate how to influence and support others to make positive health choices.

- Adapt health messages and communication techniques to a specific target audience.

Here is an overview of the preparation you'll need to do to teach each *Safe Dates* session:

SESSION TITLE	SESSION DESCRIPTION	PREPARATION NEEDED
Session 1: **Defining Caring Relationships**	Through a bingo game and class discussions, students are introduced to the *Safe Dates* program, and they consider how they'd like to be treated in dating relationships.	• *Optional:* Administer pre-test exam. • *Optional:* Print, photocopy, and mail parent letter and newsletter. • *Optional:* Purchase student "journals." • Create ground rules poster. • *Optional:* Create "How I Want to Be Treated" poster. • Purchase a prize for the winner of the Dating Bingo game. • Print and photocopy four handouts.
Session 2: **Defining Dating Abuse**	Through the discussion of scenarios and the review of statistics, students clearly define what dating abuse is.	• Post the ground rules poster. • Obtain local or state statistics on dating abuse. • Print and photocopy three handouts.
Session 3: **Why Do People Abuse?**	Through large- and small-group discussions and the review of scenarios, students identify the causes and consequences of dating abuse.	• Post the ground rules poster. • Create "Dating Abuse Red Flags" poster. • Print and photocopy three handouts.
Session 4: **How to Help Friends**	Through a decision-making exercise, a dramatic reading, and the introduction of the "Friends Wheel," students learn why it's difficult to leave abusive relationships and how to help a friend in an abusive relationship.	• Post the ground rules poster. • Make "I Want to Stay" and "I Want to Leave" signs. • Create a "Friends Wheel" poster. • Identify school staff who are trained to deal with dating abuse situations. • Gather information on local community resources that can help teens in abusive relationships. • Print and photocopy two handouts.

SESSION TITLE	SESSION DESCRIPTION	PREPARATION NEEDED
Session 5: **Helping Friends**	Through stories and role-playing, students practice skills for helping friends who are victims of abuse or confronting friends who are abusive partners.	• Post the ground rules poster. • Post the "Friends Wheel" poster. • Print and photocopy six handouts.
Session 6: **Overcoming Gender Stereotypes**	Through a writing exercise, small-group discussion, and scenarios, students learn about gender stereotypes and how these stereotypes can affect dating relationships.	• Post the ground rules poster. • Print and photocopy one handout.
Session 7: **How We Feel, How We Deal**	Through the use of a feelings diary and a discussion of "hot buttons," students learn how to recognize and effectively handle their anger, so it doesn't lead to abusive behavior.	• Post the ground rules poster. • Print and photocopy three handouts.
Session 8: **Equal Power through Communication**	Students learn the four SAFE skills for effective communication and practice these skills in a variety of role-plays.	• Post the ground rules poster. • Print and photocopy five handouts.
Session 9: **Preventing Dating Sexual Abuse**	Through taking a quiz, analysis of scenarios, and a discussion with peers, students learn about the issue of dating sexual abuse and how to prevent it from happening.	• Post the ground rules poster. • Print and photocopy three handouts. • Print, photocopy, and cut apart the Dating Tips cards. • Write scenario questions on six pieces of poster board.
Session 10: **Reviewing the *Safe Dates* Program**	Through discussion, evaluation, and a poster contest, students will review the *Safe Dates* program.	• *Optional:* Print and photocopy the post-test. • Create and photocopy a poster contest flyer. • Gather art supplies for creating posters. • Purchase prizes for poster contest winners.

SESSION 1

Defining Caring Relationships

Description

Through a bingo game and class discussions, students are introduced to the *Safe Dates* program, and they consider how they'd like to be treated in dating relationships.

Learner Outcomes

By the end of this session, students will be able to

- identify the qualities that are most important to them in a dating relationship

- identify actions that are caring and supportive

- describe how they want to be treated by a dating partner

- describe how they want to treat a dating partner

- understand that they can and should choose how they'll be treated in a dating relationship

- understand that they can and should choose how they'll treat a dating partner

**SESSION 1
AT A GLANCE**

Total Time: 50 minutes

Part 1: (12 minutes)
Introducing the
Safe Dates Curriculum
to Students

Part 2: (5 minutes)
What Is Dating?

Part 3: (8 minutes)
Dating Bingo

Part 4: Optional
(10 minutes)
Caring People and
Caring Relationships

Part 5: (8 minutes)
How I Want to
Be Treated by a
Dating Partner

Part 6: (4 minutes)
Homework Assignment

Part 7: (3 minutes)
Conclusion

Materials Needed

- ☐ *optional:* pre-test exam ⬚
- ☐ *optional:* parent letter ⬚ and parent newsletter ⬚
- ☐ *optional:* binders or three-clasp paper folders (one per student)
- ☐ *optional:* three-hole punch
- ☐ two pieces of poster board (one piece is optional)
- ☐ marker
- ☐ masking tape
- ☐ Dating Bingo cards ⬚ **Handout 1**
- ☐ pens or pencils
- ☐ an inexpensive prize for the winner of the Dating Bingo game
- ☐ *optional:* Caring People and Caring Relationships ⬚ **Handout 2**
- ☐ Ways I Want to Be Treated by a Dating Partner ⬚ **Handout 3**
- ☐ Ways I Want to Treat a Dating Partner ⬚ **Handout 4**

Preparation Needed

1. *Optional:* Print, photocopy (one for each student), and administer the pre-test exam during a class period prior to starting the *Safe Dates* program.

2. *Optional:* Print, photocopy, and mail the parent letter and parent newsletter.

3. Read this session's background information.

4. *Optional:* Purchase an inexpensive binder or three-clasp paper folder for each student to create a "journal" that holds all class handouts. Three-hole punch the handouts in every session.

5. Using a piece of poster board and a marker, list a number of ground rules you would like students to follow when discussing this sensitive topic. Post the ground rules where all students can clearly see them.

   Sample rules: confidentiality (what is said here, stays here), listen when someone is talking/no side conversations, be respectful, no criticism of others' ideas, use respectful language, you don't have to share if you don't want to.

6. *Optional:* Using the other piece of poster board, create a poster with the title "How I Want to Be Treated." Post this as well.

7. Purchase an inexpensive prize for the winner of the Dating Bingo game.

8. Print and photocopy handouts 1–4 (one for each student).

Background Information

The first session of the *Safe Dates* curriculum is designed to be fun and to help students start thinking about what they want from a dating relationship. Students will have to make a series of choices about what characteristics they want in a date, how they want to be treated, and how they want to treat a boyfriend or girlfriend. This theme about choice will echo throughout all ten sessions.

Teenagers should think about these choices *before* they begin dating. Emphasize that the *Safe Dates* program is designed both to help students in abusive relationships and to prevent teenagers from ever getting into abusive relationships. It is meant for all middle school and high school students, whether or not they have started dating.

S E S S I O N ❶ O U T L I N E

PART 1
12 minutes

▶ **Introducing the *Safe Dates* Curriculum to Students**

The purpose of part 1 is to introduce the *Safe Dates* program and to establish a safe atmosphere for discussion. Students should be reassured that the *Safe Dates* program applies to everyone, whether or not they're dating. The activities in this curriculum can help students who are not dating yet to think about issues that will prepare them for future dating.

1. Explain to students:

   We're going to meet for ten sessions to work through a program called *Safe Dates*, which is a program for preventing dating relationships from becoming abusive. We'll be discussing the following topics:

   • **how you want to be treated by a dating partner**

   • **how you want to treat a dating partner**

   • **abusive dating relationships**

   • **how you can tell if you're in an abusive dating relationship**

   • **how to help a friend who is in an abusive dating relationship**

   • **how to handle feelings like anger and jealousy**

   • **how to communicate and solve problems so relationships are healthy, not abusive**

   Each of you has a different amount of experience with dating. Many of you aren't dating at all yet, while others have been going out for a long time. The things we talk about over the next nine sessions will be important for everyone because they're about setting up healthy, happy, and fun relationships.

2. *Optional:* Pass out the *Safe Dates* journals and remind students to bring their journals to each session so they can put new handouts in them.

Teacher's Tip ✓

Adapt the wording of this introduction if you are going to be teaching the curriculum for only four or six sessions.

Teacher's Tip ✓

Collect the journals after each session to ensure that they'll be available each session.

3. Acknowledge that the subject of dating abuse is sometimes difficult to talk about because it involves close personal relationships. Briefly discuss each of the ground rules on the poster that you created. Emphasize the importance of confidentiality (what is said here, stays here).

4. Ask students if they can think of any additional ground rules. Write these on the poster board too.

5. Keep the ground rules posted so they can be referred to throughout the remaining nine sessions.

6. Explain:

   Today, we'll explore all kinds of caring relationships to see what they're "made of."

PART 2
5 minutes

▶ **What Is Dating?**

The purpose of part 2 is to help students realize that in the *Safe Dates* curriculum, the term "dating" includes informal activities such as going to the mall, going to a movie with a group of friends, listening to music at someone's house, or going swimming together.

Part 2 is designed to get students "into" the program. In this section the phrase "dating relationship" is used. Feel free to substitute a more appropriate or more readily understandable term or slang used by students.

1. Begin by asking students to define what dating is to them.

2. Explain:

   There are many different types of dating. A date may mean different things to different people.

3. Ask:

   What activities are examples of dating?

Allow students to brainstorm for a few minutes. If the less formal types of dating aren't mentioned, tell the class that going to the mall or for a walk in the park may also be considered dating.

4. Explain:

   The term "dating" in the *Safe Dates* curriculum refers to all of these activities, even the very informal ones.

PART 3
8 minutes

▶ **Dating Bingo**

The purpose of part 3 is to get students thinking about dating and making choices about dating.

1. Explain:

   To begin thinking about dating we're going to play a game called Dating Bingo.

⬚ **Handout 1**

2. Pass out a Dating Bingo card (handout 1) and a pen or pencil (if needed) to each student.

3. Explain:

   Read each of the boxes on your Dating Bingo card carefully. Then circle the five boxes that describe the qualities or characteristics you think are most important in someone you'd date. Don't talk to anyone while you're making your selections. Take a few minutes to really think about the characteristics you want in a dating partner.

4. Give students approximately two minutes to circle the items on their Dating Bingo cards.

Teacher's Tip ✓

Offer an inexpensive prize that will be highly desired by students (such as a CD or candy). It will increase their motivation to play.

5. Explain:

   Now that everyone has finished choosing their five most important characteristics of a date, get up and find someone who has circled the same qualities or characteristics.

When you find someone with the same selection, have him or her sign the box.

Your goal is to find a different person to sign each of the boxes you've circled. The first person to find a *different person* to sign all five boxes shouts "Bingo." The winner gets _____ *(describe the prize)*.

Teacher's Tip ✓

Expect the class to be noisy. If no one has called "Bingo" after five minutes, allow students to get more than one signature from the same person. Another way to shorten the activity is to have students circle three instead of five characteristics.

6. Give students approximately five minutes to walk around the room and collect signatures.

7. Check the card of the first student who shouts "Bingo" to ensure that all of the signatures are from different people. Award the prize.

PART 4
10 minutes

OPTIONAL

▶ **Caring People and Caring Relationships**

The purpose of part 4 is to allow students to explore relationships that make them feel good about themselves. Through this process, students will begin to identify ways that they enjoy being treated.

1. Explain:

    Dating Bingo was supposed to give you a chance to think about what characteristics are important to you in a dating relationship. Caring people are in all different parts of our lives. Take a moment to think about the caring people in your life who help you feel good about yourself.

🗋 Handout 2

2. Give each student a copy of handout 2, Caring People and Caring Relationships.

3. Read out loud the following instructions for "Entry One" on the handout:

    List people in your life who have helped you feel good about yourself. These people may be family members or friends. They may have been in your life for a short time

Duplicating this page is illegal. Do not copy this material without written permission from the publisher.

37

or for a long time. They may be part of your life right now, or they may not be part of your life anymore. You can list names or the person's relationship to you (such as father, mother, or history teacher).

No one will see this list except you.

4. Give students approximately two minutes to list caring people in their lives.

5. Read out loud the following instructions for "Entry Two" on the handout:

   You have written down the names of some people who have helped you feel good about yourself. Now think about what these people did to help you feel this way. Describe some of the ways they treated you.

6. Give students approximately five minutes to complete the handout.

7. After the students have finished writing, ask them:

   What are some ways that people have treated you that have helped you feel good about yourself?

   Make a list of students' responses on the poster board entitled "How I Want to Be Treated" or on the blackboard if you did not make a poster. Here are some responses to look for and to draw out:

   - they respected me
   - they trusted me
   - they listened to me
   - they took time to help me
   - they believed in me

8. Point out that such actions are important in all relationships, whether it's with a family member, friend, or date.

9. Keep the list posted so students can refer to it during the remaining sessions.

Teacher's Tip ✓

As you are creating the class list of "How I Want to Be Treated," probe vague answers (such as "they treated me nicely") by asking the student to explain what he or she means.

PART 5
8 minutes

▶ **How I Want to Be Treated by a Dating Partner**

The purpose of part 5 is to provide an opportunity for students to think about how they want to be treated. It's important to emphasize that they can decide how they'll allow others to treat them.

1. Explain:

   Although we have different types of loving relationships, we often look for the same qualities in the people we want close to us. We all want people to respect our opinions, to encourage our dreams, and to support us in hard times. So even though our relationships with our parents, our best friend, and our dating partner are different, there is a similarity in that caring people treat us in ways that help us feel good about ourselves.

   Perhaps there are special ways you want to be treated by your dating partner. The next exercise will help you think about the ways you want to be treated by the person you're dating.

🖉 **Handout 3**

2. Pass out handout 3, Ways I Want to Be Treated by a Dating Partner (one copy per student).

3. Explain:

   This handout features a figure and a list of ways dating partners may treat each other. The figure represents *you*. On the two solid lines next to the figure, write the *two most important* ways you want to be treated by a dating partner. This is your bottom line. *Bottom line* means they are the two things you *must* have in a relationship.

   No relationship is perfect. It's important to think about what's most important to you, however, because you do have some power and control over how you're treated.

   On the five dotted lines farther away from the figure, write five other ways you want to be treated. Feel free to write ideas that aren't on the list. You will *not* have to share this information with anyone if you don't want to.

4. Give the students a few minutes to read through the list and think about their own experience before they write anything in the blanks. Allow them time to fill in the handout.

5. If there is time, ask:

    Would anyone like to share the two most important ways they want to be treated?

    Allow several students the opportunity to share.

6. Explain:

    When you're dating someone, go over this list every once in a while to see if you're getting the things that are most important to you in the relationship. We all have choices in how we're treated. *If you aren't getting the things that are most important to you, you have choices to make about the relationship.*

PART 6
4 minutes

▶ **Homework Assignment**

The purpose of part 6 is to provide an opportunity for students to think about how they want to treat a girlfriend or boyfriend. It's important to emphasize that they can make active decisions about how they treat their dating partners too.

1. Explain:

    In addition to having the right to choose how you want to be treated *by* others, you have the ability to choose how you treat other people. Every day we all make choices about how we interact with others. In the following sessions, we'll spend a great deal of time talking about positive ways to interact with other people.

    As homework, I'd like you to think about how you *want* to treat a dating partner. This assignment asks you to choose five ways that you want to treat someone you are or someday may be dating.

Handout 4

2. Pass out a copy of handout 4, Ways I Want to Treat a Dating Partner (one per student).

3. Read the following instructions out loud:

   The handout features two figures and a list of ways dating partners may treat each other. The figure on the left represents *you*. The figure on the right represents *your dating partner*. There are five lines that run from you to your dating partner. On these lines, write in the ways you want to treat a dating partner. Feel free to write in characteristics that aren't on the list.

4. Ask students to complete the homework assignment before the next class. Tell the students that you won't look at their responses but will check to make sure the homework is completed.

PART 7
3 minutes

▶ **Conclusion**

1. Summarize the session by saying:

   - **You can choose how you want to be treated by a dating partner.**

   - **You make choices in the way you act toward your dating partner.**

   - **In the next nine sessions we are going to talk about what you can do if you aren't being treated the way you want to be, how to tell if behavior is abusive, and how to prevent abuse in a dating relationship.**

   - **All of you are at different stages when it comes to dating. Some of you are already dating and some of you are not dating at all. This curriculum is for each of you. Even if you are not yet dating, someday you will be, and *Safe Dates* can help prepare you to prevent and recognize dating abuse.**

   - *Optional:* **Put today's handouts in your journal and bring your journal with you next session** (or collect the journals for next time).

SESSION 2

Defining Dating Abuse

Description

Through the discussion of scenarios and the review of statistics, students clearly define what dating abuse is.

Learner Outcomes

By the end of this session, students will be able to

- identify harmful dating behaviors

- define physically and emotionally abusive behaviors

- identify physical and emotional abuse in dating relationships

- be more likely to identify abusive behaviors as abusive

- be more aware of their susceptibility to dating abuse

- be more likely to reject abuse as normal in dating relationships

**SESSION 2
AT A GLANCE**

Total Time: 50 minutes

Part 1: (5 minutes)
Ground Rules and Homework

Part 2: (6 minutes)
Identifying Harmful Behaviors

Part 3: (25 minutes)
What Is Abuse?

Part 4: (7 minutes)
Defining Abusive Dating Relationships

Part 5: (5 minutes)
Facts about Dating Abuse

Part 6: (2 minutes)
Conclusion

Materials Needed

- ☐ ground rules poster (from session 1)
- ☐ *optional:* student journals (if students didn't keep them)
- ☐ masking tape
- ☐ chalkboard, dry-eraseboard, or flipchart
- ☐ chalk and/or markers
- ☐ Typical Harmful Dating Behaviors 🗒 **Handout 5**
- ☐ Defining Dating Abuse Scenarios 🗒 **Handout 6**
- ☐ Facts about Dating Abuse 🗒 **Handout 7**
- ☐ scissors
- ☐ pens or pencils

Preparation Needed

1. Read this session's background information.

2. Post the ground rules, if they aren't still up.

3. Obtain local or state statistics on dating abuse from your community's domestic violence crisis center, county mental health service, or local university. If you can't find local or state statistics, use the national statistics provided in this lesson.

4. Print and photocopy handouts 5–7 (one for each student).

Background Information

Almost everyone holds an opinion on the sensitive issues of violence and abuse in dating relationships. Sometimes a discussion about dating abuse will affect people at a very personal level. Be aware of this fact. To facilitate this second session, you'll need to be willing to hear things with which you disagree. The primary goal of the session is to stimulate a good discussion that airs many different sides of the issue.

Session 2 begins by asking the students to list harmful behaviors. Starting with harmful instead of abusive behaviors makes two subtle points: First, the meaning of the word "harmful" implies the consequences of actions. Second, the students are likely to think of behaviors that are painful but not necessarily abusive. This list will help you later differentiate between normal conflict in a relationship and abuse.

Throughout the session's discussions, many controversial issues may arise. Although it may feel uncomfortable not to personally address each issue, your role as facilitator is to bring out all opinions around the definition of abuse and to explain the definition used in the *Safe Dates* program (see part 4). There are bound to be loose ends at the end of the session when covering such a complicated topic in only fifty minutes.

SESSION 2 OUTLINE

PART 1
5 minutes

▶ **Ground Rules and Homework**

The purpose of part 1 is to review the ground rules and to briefly talk about the homework assignment from session 1.

1. Explain:

    To start out the session, we're going to review our ground rules and talk about your homework assignment from session 1.

2. Ask one of the students to read the ground rules (they should be posted in your classroom).

3. Ask:

    Does anyone have any ground rules to add today?

    Add any suggested ground rules to the list.

4. Briefly explain your policy on reporting dating abuse or other violence being done by or to students. State this policy up front so students don't feel set up or betrayed if they reveal abusive situations to you.

5. Explain:

    Your homework assignment was to think about how you want to treat a dating partner.

    If you have time, ask:

    Would anyone like to share how he or she wants to treat a dating partner?

    Allow a few students to share.

Teacher's Tip ✓

If students share negative ideas to get attention, don't make a big deal of it. Just say, "That's too bad" and move on to the next student.

6. Explain:

    Remember, even if you are not yet dating, *Safe Dates* can help you prevent and recognize dating abuse when you do start dating. What you learn here will definitely help you in the future.

7. *Optional:* Check off whether students completed their homework.

PART 2
6 minutes

▶ **Identifying Harmful Behaviors**

The purpose of part 2 is to acknowledge a broad spectrum of harmful behaviors that occur in dating relationships.

1. Explain:

   In the last session, we talked about qualities we want in all caring relationships, particularly dating relationships. Today, we'll be talking about characteristics of harmful dating relationships.

2. Write "Harmful Behaviors" on the chalkboard, dry-erase-board, or flipchart. Then draw two columns. Label one column "Physical Harm" and the other column "Emotional Harm."

Teacher's Tip ✓

If the students have a hard time thinking of harmful dating behaviors, encourage them to think about dating relationships they've seen on television or have heard about.

3. Ask the students to name things that people do in dating relationships that are harmful. Write each student's response in the appropriate column.

4. Sometimes adolescents can easily list physically harmful behaviors but neglect emotionally harmful behaviors. If the class is coming up with only physical behaviors (such as hitting, pushing, shoving, spitting, pulling hair), probe them by asking the following questions:

   • **What about threatening or spreading rumors about a dating partner?**

   • **What about making fun of a dating partner in front of his or her friends?**

   • **What other behaviors are emotionally or psychologically harmful?**

   Develop as extensive a list as possible with the students. There are no right or wrong answers in this exercise, so write down everything the students mention. A list of harmful behaviors typically mentioned by students can be found on the next page.

Duplicating this page is illegal. Do not copy this material without written permission from the publisher.

47

Typical Harmful Behaviors Mentioned by Students

PHYSICAL HARM	EMOTIONAL HARM
• hitting	• calling a dating partner names
• scratching	• criticizing opinions
• pushing	• ignoring a dating partner's feelings
• threatening	• isolating a dating partner from others
• pinching	• behaving jealously
• choking	• telling lies
• spitting	• scaring a dating partner
• shaking	• cheating on a dating partner
• shoving	• making a dating partner feel guilty
• forcing	• spreading rumors
• biting	• threatening to hurt a dating partner
• pulling hair	• threatening to hurt oneself
• using a weapon	• using sexually derogatory names
• throwing things	• criticizing beliefs about sex
• keeping a dating partner from leaving	• putting down family and friends
• molestation	• driving recklessly to scare a dating partner
• rape	• humiliating a dating partner in public or private
• forcing unwanted sexual actions	• insulting a dating partner's beliefs or values
• damaging personal property	• displaying inappropriate anger
• acting in an intimidating way	
• purposefully injuring an animal	

Handout 5

5. Distribute handout 5, Typical Harmful Dating Behaviors, and encourage students to refer to this list as they date others.

6. Ask:

   What are some ways that technology such as cell phones, e-mail, IM, text messaging, chat rooms, blogs, and social networking sites like MySpace or Facebook can be used to abuse dating partners?

   (Possible answers include sending insults, showing private and embarrassing pictures of dating partners to others, monitoring the activities of dating partners, spreading rumors about dating partners, and frightening or threatening dating partners.)

PART 3
25 minutes

▶ **What Is Abuse?**

The purpose of part 3 is to allow students to debate what abuse is and to begin to define what it means for the class.

1. Explain:

   Some behaviors seem obviously abusive, while it's difficult to decide about other behaviors, depending on what else is going on.

Handout 6

2. Pass out a copy of handout 6, Defining Dating Abuse Scenarios, to all students. Select four students. Assign each of the four students to read one of the scenarios.

Teacher's Tip ✓

If the scenarios in handout 6 do not reflect the culture of your classroom, you can modify the scenarios by changing names and including activities representative of your students.

3. One at a time, have the students read their scenarios to the class. After each scenario, ask students the question(s) that follow each scenario in this manual. Reinforce that there are no right or wrong answers in this activity.

4. Write all of the students' answers to the "Why?" questions on a chalkboard, dry-eraseboard, or flipchart. These answers will help students form their own definition of dating abuse.

SCENARIO 1: JASON AND MEGAN

Jason invited several of his friends and his girlfriend, Megan, to his house to watch movies on Friday night. Jason asked Megan if she would put out some chips and drinks for everyone. She said that she didn't mind. When Jason's friends arrived, they all sat down to watch movies.

When someone finished a drink or when the bowl of chips was empty, Jason would tell Megan to go to the kitchen for refills. When this happened for the third time, Megan said that she wouldn't be their waitress. She wanted to watch the movie, and they could help themselves to the food in the kitchen if they wanted it.

Jason got angry. He ordered Megan to get his friends' drinks. When she refused, Jason hit her across the face and pulled her into the kitchen. Jason's friends had seen Jason and Megan fight like this many times.

Scenario 1 Questions:

a. **Is Jason abusive? Why or why not?**

   Write the students' responses on the board.

b. **What if this scenario had not ended with Jason hitting Megan? Instead, Jason got angry and ordered her to get his friends' drinks. When she refused, he "got in her face" and said, "What did you say?" Megan responded by withdrawing and being quiet. Is that still abuse?**

c. **If this was the first time Jason and Megan had fought, would it still be abuse?**

Note: This scenario can also be used to encourage students to think about the difference (if there is any) between violence that happens one time and recurring violence.

Teacher's Tip ✓

This scenario may be used to point out both physical and emotional abuse.

SCENARIO 2: CHRISTINA AND JUAN

Christina and Juan have been dating for a few weeks. Juan likes Christina, but he isn't in love with her. He wants to date another girl in his health class. When he tells Christina that he wants to break up, she gets angry. Then she starts crying. Juan is uncomfortable. He doesn't know what to say, but he doesn't want to be in a relationship with Christina anymore.

Scenario 2 Question:

a. Is Juan abusive? Why or why not?

Write the students' responses on the board.

Teacher's Tip ✓

This scenario can be used to point out that not all harmful behaviors and conflicts are necessarily abusive.

Note: Dating may involve difficult and painful experiences, but those experiences aren't always abusive. Misunderstandings and thoughtlessness may make a person feel bad, but such conflicts can be resolved in a way that allows both people to express themselves.

SCENARIO 3: TYRONE AND NICOLE

Tyrone bought Nicole an iTunes gift card for her birthday so she could buy new music for her iPod. Nicole opened the gift card and at first she seemed to love the gift. Then, however, she asked where the rest of her gifts were. When Tyrone said that he just got the iTunes gift card for her birthday present, Nicole got angry. She started screaming at him. She said that she expected more than a stupid gift card for her birthday, and she threw the gift card across the room.

Scenario 3 Question:

a. Is Nicole abusive? Why or why not?

Write the students' responses on the board.

Teacher's Tip ✓

This scenario can be used to point out that guys can be hurt by their girlfriends' abusive behaviors too.

Note: You could read the scenario again, switching Tyrone's and Nicole's names, and ask the students how they feel when the roles are changed.

You may want to add at this point that all kinds of people suffer from abuse in dating relationships: girls and boys; whites, African Americans, Native Americans, Hispanics, and Asians; students born in rich neighborhoods and students born in poor neighborhoods; people who come from abusive homes and people who do not; people who have dated a lot and people who have just begun dating.

SCENARIO 4: TAU AND LU

Teacher's Tip ✓

This scenario can be used to show that not all controlling behaviors are violent or obvious. By making Tau feel guilty, Lu is isolating her from her friends. However, his tactics may make him *seem* "sweet." And it may *seem* as if the problem is with Tau.

Tau has a group of very close girlfriends. She enjoys going to movies and the mall with them. When she met Lu and they fell in love, the couple began spending every spare minute together— that was three months ago. All of Tau's friends like Lu, but they miss being able to spend time with Tau. Tau would like to go out with them as well. But every time she tells Lu that she's going out with her girlfriends, Lu tells her how much he misses her when she's gone, that he always wants her by his side. And when Tau does go out with her friends, Lu constantly calls and texts her. If she doesn't answer her cell or her texts from Lu, he gets angry and accuses Tau of wanting to be with her friends more than him. Tau loves Lu and she never wants to hurt him. As a result, though, she feels too guilty to leave Lu even for a few hours to spend time with her old friends.

Scenario 4 Questions:

a. Is Lu abusive? Why or why not?

Write the students' responses on the board.

b. Is Tau abusive? Why or why not?

Write the students' responses on the board.

Note: You may also point out that dating abuse situations aren't typically "cut and dry." The person may be wonderful, supportive, and romantic most of the time, but in just one or two situations she or he is controlling or manipulative.

PART 4
7 minutes

▶ **Defining Abusive Dating Relationships**

The purpose of part 4 is to distinguish when harmful behaviors are abusive.

1. Explain:

   Based on what we just talked about in these four scenarios, I'd like to define "dating abuse."

Summarize the key points from your discussion, including the following:

- Harmful behaviors are abusive when . . .

    a. they're used to *manipulate*

    b. they're used to *gain control*

    c. they're used to *gain power over* someone

    d. they make you *feel bad* about yourself or other people you're close to (friends, family, and so on)

    e. they make you *afraid* of your dating partner

- An abusive dating partner can use physical or emotional attacks.

- Emotional, sexual, and physical dating abuse are all serious.

2. Bring the students' attention back to the list of harmful behaviors they created at the beginning of this session.

3. Explain:

    When emotional abuse (such as behaving jealously, making someone feel guilty, or insulting someone) happens once, it may not be abusive. It becomes a problem when these actions happen more than once and when they're used to manipulate, control, gain power over someone, or make a person feel bad. Any use of physical or sexual violence, however, is abusive, even if it's done only once.

Teacher's Tip ✓

Use current events to discuss dating abuse. Take the time to discuss media stories about celebrities or people in your community who have been involved with dating abuse. It's helpful for students to know that dating abuse can happen to/ with anybody.

PART 5

5 minutes

▶ **Facts about Dating Abuse**

The purpose of part 5 is to give students factual information about dating abuse. This information contradicts common perceptions about abuse in dating relationships and portrays dating abuse as a serious and pervasive problem in our society.

🖳 **Handout 7**

1. Distribute handout 7, Facts about Dating Abuse. The following national statistics are also on the handout. Encourage students to take turns reading these statistics aloud.

- **In the United States, about 12 percent of high school students report having been physically victimized by a dating partner in the previous year.[1] In some areas of the country, this is as high as 40 percent.[2]**

- **About one in four high school students report having been psychologically abused by a dating partner in the previous year.[3]**

- **Gay male and female adolescents are victims of physical and psychological dating abuse about as often as heterosexual adolescents.**

- **Dating abuse is beginning as early as the sixth grade.[4]**

- **Adults who use violence with their dating partners often begin doing so during adolescence, with the first episode typically occurring by age fifteen.[5]**

- **Young women between the ages of fourteen and seventeen represent 38 percent of those victimized by date rape.[6]**

- **Many research studies show that, by far, the majority of adolescents believe that being abusive to dates is wrong and should not be done.**

2. Share any local statistics you can find on dating abuse. Local statistics may have a greater impact on students than national statistics. The state-specific Youth Risk Behavior Surveys, conducted by the Centers for Disease Control and Prevention, include questions on dating abuse. Check the CDC Web site to determine if that survey was conducted in your state.

3. Also share the following key concepts:

- **Both girls and boys are victims of dating abuse, though girls receive more severe injuries from dating abuse than boys.**

- **Both girls and boys are perpetrators of dating abuse, though girls tend to use less severe forms of dating abuse than boys.**

- **Teenagers from all neighborhoods, income levels, and ethnic groups experience abuse in dating relationships.**

- **Dating abuse can happen to anyone in any relationship.**

- **Abuse almost always recurs in a relationship. It doesn't just go away.**

- **Most abuse gets more severe over time.**

PART 6
2 minutes

▶ **Conclusion**

1. Explain:

   Everyone needs to know how to deal with dating abuse for two primary reasons: (1) in case they end up in an abusive relationship themselves; and (2) in case a friend in an abusive relationship turns to them for help.

   Knowing how you want to be treated will help you determine whether you're in an abusive relationship. Use your own list of harmful behaviors as warning signs for abuse. If you aren't being treated the way you want to be, then you have some choices to make about the relationship.

2. *Optional:* Have students add all session 2 handouts to their journals. Remind them to bring their journals to the next session (if you don't collect them).

Notes

1. Centers for Disease Control and Prevention, "Youth Risk Behavior Surveillance—United States, 2007," *Surveillance Summaries, MMWR 2008*; 57 (No. SS-4).

2. V. A. Foshee and R. Matthew, "Adolescent Dating Abuse Perpetration: A Review of Findings, Methodological Limitations, and Suggestions for Future Research," in *The Cambridge Handbook of Violent Behavior and Aggression,* ed. Daniel Flannery, Alexander Vazsonyi, and I. Waldman (New York: Cambridge University Press, 2007).

3. C. T. Halpern, M. L. Young, M. W. Waller, S. L. Martin, and L. L. Kupper, "Prevalence of Partner Violence in Same-Sex Romantic and Sexual Relationships in a National Sample of Adolescents," *Journal of Adolescent Health* 35, no. 2 (2004): 124–31. Carolyn Tucker Halpern, Selene G. Oslak, Mary L. Young, Sandra L. Martin, and Lawrence L. Kupper, "Partner Violence among Adolescents in Opposite-Sex Romantic Relationships: Findings from the National Longitudinal Study of Adolescent Health," *American Journal of Public Health* 91, no. 10 (October 2001).

4. S. Miller-Johnson, D. Gorman-Smith, T. Sullivan, P. Orpinas, T. R. Simon, "Parent and Peer Predictors of Physical Dating Violence Perpetration in Early Adolescence: Tests of Moderation and Gender Differences," *Journal of Clinical Child and Adolescent Psychology* 38, no. 4 (2009): 538–50. B. Taylor, N. Stein, A. R. Mack, T. J. Horwood, and F. Burden, *Experimental Evaluation of Gender Violence/Harassment Prevention Programs in Middle Schools. Final Report.* (National Institute of Justice, 2008).

5. J. Henton, R. Cate, J. Koval, S. Lloyd, and S. Christopher, "Romance and Violence in Dating Relationships," *Journal of Family Issues* 4, no. 3 (1983): 467–82.

6. Robin Warshaw, *I Never Called It Rape: The Ms. Report on Recognizing, Fighting and Surviving Date and Acquaintance Rape* (New York: Harper and Row, 1988).

SESSION 3

Why Do People Abuse?

Description

Through large- and small-group discussions and the review of scenarios, students identify the causes and consequences of dating abuse.

Learner Outcomes

By the end of this session, students will be able to

- describe the controlling and manipulative functions of dating abuse
- identify abusive behaviors as abusive
- choose not to believe common misperceptions of why dating abuse happens
- understand that dating abuse is a serious matter
- understand that abuse is not the victim's fault
- describe the serious short- and long-term consequences of abusive relationships
- identify the warning signs that a person is a victim of abuse or is an abusive partner

SESSION 3 AT A GLANCE

Total Time: 50 minutes

Part 1: (15 minutes)
People Abuse to Control and Manipulate Someone

Part 2: (10 minutes)
Other Reasons for Abuse

Part 3: (15 minutes)
Consequences of Dating Abuse

Part 4: (7 minutes)
Warning Signs of Abuse

Part 5: (3 minutes)
Conclusion

Duplicating this page is illegal. Do not copy this material without written permission from the publisher.

57

Materials Needed

☐ ground rules poster (from session 1)

☐ *optional:* student journals (if students didn't keep them)

☐ chalkboard, dry-eraseboard, or flipchart

☐ chalk and/or markers

☐ Why People Abuse Scenarios   **Handout 8**

☐ The Consequences of Dating Abuse   **Handouts 9A, 9B, 9C**

☐ poster board

☐ masking tape

☐ Dating Abuse Red Flags   **Handout 10**

Preparation Needed

1. Read this session's background information.

2. Post the ground rules, if they aren't still up.

3. Print and photocopy handouts 8–10 (one for each student).

4. Using poster board and a marker, create a poster entitled "Dating Abuse Red Flags." Write some examples of dating abuse red flags on the poster. Examples are provided on pages 69–70. Write "Red Flags for Victims" and "Red Flags for Abusive Partners" in separate columns.

Background Information

The primary purpose of session 3 is to help students recognize that abusive dating behaviors are controlling. When someone is in an abusive relationship, it's often difficult to see the partner's behavior as manipulative. Many times victims see their partner's behavior as uncontrollable anger, jealousy, or insecurity. If students can identify the manipulative aspect of behaviors in a story, they're more likely to see similar behaviors as manipulative in their own lives.

The exercises in this session involve class discussion and group work, giving students a structured and positive environment to talk about abuse with their peers. Here students can address norms that perpetuate abuse and talk about the negative impact of such behaviors.

These discussions may be challenging to facilitate. As the teacher, you may want to refer to the suggestions found in the introduction (pages 13–15).

Duplicating this page is illegal. Do not copy this material without written permission from the publisher.

59

SESSION 3 OUTLINE

At the beginning of this session, spend a few minutes reviewing the ground rules.

PART 1
15 minutes

▶ **People Abuse to Control and Manipulate Someone**

The purpose of part 1 is to help students recognize that abusive behaviors are used to control and manipulate the way a person acts, feels, and thinks. Being aware of the manipulative and controlling function of abuse may enable students to protect themselves.

1. Explain:

    During session 1 we talked about caring relationships. We talked about the ways that you want to be treated by a dating partner, and the ways that you want to treat a dating partner. During session 2 we talked about abusive behaviors, both emotional and physical, and the negative effects such behaviors may have on individuals.

    Today, we're going to talk about why people abuse. If most people want to be treated and treat others with love, kindness, and respect, then why are there abusive relationships?

2. Write "Why Do People Abuse?" on the chalkboard, dry-eraseboard, or flipchart.

3. Explain:

    We're going to read three scenarios and I'm going to ask you some questions about them so we can try to figure out why people abuse others.

4. Ask for three student volunteers. Give each volunteer the three Why People Abuse Scenarios (handout 8). Give a copy of all three scenarios to the rest of the class as well.

🖺 **Handout 8**

Have a volunteer read scenario 1 out loud:

SCENARIO 1:
PEOPLE ABUSE TO CONTROL THE WAY SOMEONE ACTS

Hee-Jung and Michael have just started dating. Michael doesn't know all of Hee-Jung's friends. As he walks out of school in the afternoon, he sees Hee-Jung talking to Jon. It looks like a private conversation and Hee-Jung is laughing. Michael thinks she is flirting and becomes angry. He walks over to Hee-Jung, puts his arm around her, and says, "Let's go," as he pulls her away. Hee-Jung tries to introduce Michael and Jon, but Michael cuts her off, saying, "I said, let's go now." Michael drags Hee-Jung away. He leaves a bruise on her arm. Hee-Jung tries to explain that Jon is her older brother's best friend. They've known each other since they were small children. She wasn't flirting. Michael says he won't have his girlfriend embarrassing him in front of the entire school by talking to other guys. Later that evening, Michael goes to Hee-Jung's house with a dozen roses and tells her that he loves her very much. That's why it drives him crazy when she talks to other guys.

5. Ask students the following questions:

a. **How does Michael want Hee-Jung to act?**

(Possible answers: to not talk with any other guys; to be committed; like she is his possession; to know what he wants; to put his needs before hers; Michael wants Hee-Jung all to himself)

Teacher's Tip ✓

Students may say, "because he loves her" in response to question b. If you hear this response, point out that Michael may love Hee-Jung, but controlling someone doesn't show love.

b. **Why might Michael want Hee-Jung to act this way?**

(Possible answers: because he is insecure; because he's arrogant; to make him feel he has power; to make him feel comfortable/less insecure)

c. **How is Michael getting Hee-Jung to act this way?**

(Possible answers: by automatically accusing her; by giving her roses; by putting his arm around her and pulling her away; by saying it's embarrassing; by making her behavior seem inappropriate and his behavior seem appropriate)

6. Explain:

   Michael is being abusive by trying to control the way Hee-Jung *acts*.

7. Write "To control the way someone acts" on the board.

8. Explain:

   Scenario 1 is about jealousy:

   a. **When you like someone a lot, you'll probably feel jealous sometimes. It isn't wrong or unusual to feel jealous, but limiting the people your dating partner can talk to *is* abusive.**

   b. **Having a dating partner who's so jealous that she or he doesn't want you to talk to other people may seem flattering at first, but it's actually a way of manipulating and controlling you. If a relationship like this continues, it's likely that the victim, in this case Hee-Jung, will become isolated from friends and family.**

   c. **One way that people can control the way their dating partner acts is to pair abusive behavior with nice behavior. In this scenario, Michael brought Hee-Jung roses after he abused her. This common behavior by abusive people "hooks" the victim even more. Seeing a person be sweet makes it hard to leave him or her, and that's why the nice things like bringing flowers and gifts can be manipulative.**

   d. **One reason people may be abusive is to control the way their dating partner *acts*.**

9. Have a second volunteer read scenario 2 out loud:

SCENARIO 2:
PEOPLE ABUSE TO CONTROL THE WAY SOMEONE FEELS

Mario and Cassie have been dating for about a month. One Saturday night, Mario borrows his brother's car and comes to pick Cassie up to go to the movies. Cassie meets him at the door in a new outfit. Mario gives her a kiss and then asks if she's going to change before they go out.

Cassie almost cries. She explains that she bought this outfit just for their date tonight. Mario sighs, pats her on the shoulder, and says, "Cassie, no one else would ever put up with you. I don't know why I love you so much. I have to do everything for you." Then he goes up to Cassie's room and chooses a different outfit.

10. Ask students the following questions:

   a. **How does Mario want Cassie to feel?**

      (Possible answers: bad about herself; dependent, like she needs Mario to take care of her; insecure; helpless; useless)

   b. **Why might Mario want Cassie to feel this way?**

      (Possible answers: because she'll be less likely to leave him; so that he has more control; so he feels powerful)

   c. **How does Mario get Cassie to feel this way?**

      (Possible answers: by putting her down, but also saying he's there for her; by trying to convince her that no one else would want to date her)

11. Explain:

   Another reason that people may abuse their boyfriend or girlfriend is to control the way she or he *feels*.

12. Write "To control the way someone feels" on the board.

13. Explain:

   Some people excuse abuse by saying they're only trying to help their girlfriend or boyfriend to be more popular, to use her or his time more wisely, or to keep her or him safe. As the relationship continues and this behavior gets worse, the controlling partner may interfere in personal decisions about school, clothing, family, and friends.

Often, people who abuse want their boyfriend or girlfriend to feel bad about himself or herself and dependent on the dating partner and, therefore, less likely to leave. In this scenario, Mario is pairing abuse with kindness ("I love you so much") in a manipulative way.

So, sometimes people abuse to control the way someone *acts* and sometimes people abuse to control the way someone *feels*.

14. Have a third volunteer read scenario 3 out loud:

SCENARIO 3:
PEOPLE ABUSE TO CONTROL
THE WAY SOMEONE THINKS

Mickey and Chris have been dating for several months. They've been having a number of disagreements lately. Chris is angry and frustrated. Things between them don't seem like they'll ever get better.

Chris has been confiding in a friend, Drew. Chris's friendship with Drew makes Mickey jealous, causing even more fights. Last week, Chris told Mickey that this relationship might not work. Mickey said that if he would stop flirting and cheating with Drew, the fighting would stop and they could be happy again. Chris said Drew was just a friend, but it didn't really matter because if they weren't fighting about Mickey's jealousy, they were fighting about something else.

That night, Mickey called Chris. She was crying and saying things like, "I need you and I couldn't stand to lose you to someone else. You are the best part of my life. If you take that happiness away from me, I'll hurt myself." Since then, Mickey has called and sent texts to Chris, saying, "I'll hurt myself if you leave me." Chris feels trapped.

15. Ask students the following questions:

a. **How does Mickey want Chris to feel?**

(Possible answers: bad; responsible for her actions; confused; guilty; sorry for her)

Teacher's Tip ✓

The couple in scenario 3 could be either a heterosexual couple or a same-sex couple. If you decide to read it as a same-sex couple, eliminate the pronouns and replace with the names.

b. What does Mickey want Chris to think?

(Possible answers: the abuse is his fault; she needs him)

c. Why does Mickey want Chris to think and feel this way?

(Possible answers: so she doesn't have to feel bad about what she does; she doesn't want Chris to leave the relationship)

d. How does Mickey get Chris to think and feel this way?

(Possible answers: by blaming Chris for the abuse; by making him feel sorry for her; by threatening self-harm if he leaves; by making him feel responsible for "saving" her)

16. Explain:

    Often, people who abuse try to blame the abuse on the victim and try to make the victim think that it's his or her fault. Making the victim feel responsible for the partner's harmful actions is manipulative. If the victim thinks the abuse is her or his fault, then

    a. he or she will try harder and harder to please the abusive partner

    b. the victim will not see the abusive partner as bad

    c. the abusive partner doesn't have to take any responsibility for his or her actions

    A third reason why people may abuse is to control the way their dating partner *thinks*.

17. Write "To control the way someone thinks" on the board.

18. Explain:

    Sometimes people who abuse want the victim to feel sorry for them. They want the victim to think she or he is needed to save or help the dating partner. If the victim feels sorry for his or her dating partner or feels a need to help him or her, then the victim will be less likely to leave the relationship. When an abusive person makes a dating partner feel like he or she has to stay in the relationship, it's controlling and manipulative.

19. Summarize by saying:

Some of the reasons that a person may abuse a dating partner are to control the way that person acts, feels, and thinks.

PART 2
10 minutes

▶ **Other Reasons for Abuse**

If you are running low on time for this session, this part can be skipped.

1. Explain:

Each of the three scenarios highlights a reason people may be abusive. The desire to control and manipulate the way a dating partner acts, feels, and thinks is a common reason for abuse. Here are some other reasons why people abuse. (If you have time, write these on the board as well.)

a. because they believe it's the "normal" way to act

b. because expectations and feelings of insecurity make them think they need power over others

c. because they've learned that they can get what they want by abusing

d. because they don't know other (nonviolent) ways of responding to anger, frustration, or conflict

e. because they have underdeveloped communication skills, which cause anger, resentment, and frustration to build up

f. because they're using alcohol or other illicit drugs, which sometimes causes people to become abusive or to do things they'd otherwise never do (such as commit date rape)

Teacher's Tip ✓

If students suggest that people abuse because they're mad at their girlfriend or boyfriend, stress that there are other ways of responding when you're angry. It's okay to be angry, but people have a choice whether to be abusive.

PART 3
15 minutes

▶ **Consequences of Dating Abuse**

The purpose of part 3 is to have students make a connection between an abusive act and the consequences of that act for the victim and the abusive partner. When students grasp the extent of harm that abusive and violent behaviors cause, they'll begin to understand why it's important to learn better ways of dealing with relationship problems.

You'll want students to work in groups of no more than four people. If you have more than twelve students in your class, some groups will have to discuss the same dating abuse situations.

1. Explain:

    We've thought about why people abuse other people. Now, let's discuss the effect this abuse has on both the victim and the abusive partner. Although an abusive act—a slap or an insult, for example—may last only a split second, the consequences of that act are likely to last much, much longer.

2. Explain:

    There are two types of consequences: short-term and long-term. Short-term consequences are immediate and happen during or right after the abuse. An example of a short-term consequence is feeling humiliated when your dating partner yells at you in front of your friends. Long-term consequences happen later that day, the next day, the next week, the next year, or even many years afterward when a teen becomes an adult. When a person stays for a long time in a relationship where abusive behavior is happening, a long-term consequence for the victim might be having little to no self-esteem and an inability to have healthy relationships with family members, friends, and dating partners.

    I'm going to divide you into groups of three or four people. The first thing to do in your group is to choose a

Duplicating this page is illegal. Do not copy this material without written permission from the publisher.

67

Teacher's Tip ✓

If you have several small groups, select just a few recorders to report to the whole group.

"recorder," someone who will write down your group's answers and present them to the whole class. I'll be passing out a handout listing harmful behaviors. Each group will discuss the consequences of the behaviors for the girl and the boy.

3. Break the students into small groups.

4. Give each group a few minutes to select a recorder.

☐ **Handouts 9A, 9B, 9C**

Give each student The Consequences of Dating Abuse handouts (9A, 9B, and 9C). Assign the groups to work on just one of the handouts (9A, 9B, or 9C). Give the groups about eight minutes to work together. If you are running low on time, have the students work on just one or two of the consequences on their assigned handout.

5. After the groups are done discussing the behaviors, ask the recorders to briefly summarize their group's discussion.

PART 4
7 minutes

▶ **Warning Signs of Abuse**

The purpose of part 4 is to help students identify warning signs of an abusive or potentially abusive relationship.

1. Explain:

   Too often, a relationship becomes very painful and even dangerous before anyone seeks help. Certain feelings and behaviors, however, can alert you to an abusive relationship. Today, we're going to call these feelings and behaviors "red flags." In a relationship, red flags can be seen as warning signs that changes need to be made before things get dangerous.

2. Put up your prepared list of red flags on poster board (one column for victims and the other for abusive partners).

☐ **Handout 10**

3. Pass out handout 10, Dating Abuse Red Flags (one copy for each student).

4. Ask student volunteers to read aloud each item on the handout.

5. Explain:

    People may have different or additional red flags. Can anyone think of other feelings or behaviors that indicate a relationship might grow to be abusive?

6. Add students' ideas to the red flags poster. Hang the poster in the classroom so students can refer to it later.

Red flags for people who may be in an abusive relationship

- being physically hurt
- feeling afraid of your dating partner
- feeling isolated, maybe even alone
- losing your friends
- changing your behavior because of your dating partner's jealousy
- feeling embarrassed, put down, ashamed, or guilty
- being threatened
- feeling manipulated or controlled
- being afraid to express your own feelings of anger
- feeling a nervous or sick feeling in your stomach when your dating partner is irritated, frustrated, or angry
- feeling a pounding or fluttering in your chest when your dating partner isn't happy
- not being allowed to, or being afraid to, make decisions for yourself
- noticing that your dating partner has very traditional (stereotypical) beliefs about women and men
- noticing that your dating partner's beliefs about the position of men and women in society are different from your own
- feeling as if your dating partner gets too personal or touches you in an unwanted way
- not having your thoughts or wishes for personal space respected

Red flags for people who may be abusing their dating partner

- physically assaulting your dating partner (hitting, slapping, pushing, kicking)
- intimidating your dating partner
- becoming angry if your dating partner is spending time with other people
- asking your dating partner to change his or her behavior because you're jealous
- verbally threatening your dating partner
- using "guilt trips" to get your dating partner to do something
- feeling unable to control your own feelings of anger
- making your dating partner afraid of you
- forcing your dating partner to do sexual things that he or she is not comfortable doing

PART 5
3 minutes

▶ **Conclusion**

1. Summarize this session by sharing the following key points:
   - **People act abusively for many different reasons.**
   - **Abusive behaviors have serious short- and long-term consequences for the victim and the abusive partner.**
   - **There are usually red flags, or warning signs, that a person may be abusive or abused.**
   - **All of the scenarios that we read today could have ended differently. People can choose to act in cooperative, non-abusive ways. For this reason, it's never the victim's fault that she or he has gotten hit, insulted, or threatened.**

   No one ever deserves to be abused.

2. *Optional:* Consider posting the list of red flags in your hallways, bathrooms, or other school locations.

3. *Optional:* Have students add all session 3 handouts to their journals. Remind them to bring their journals to the next session (if you don't collect them).

SESSION 4

How to Help Friends

Description

Through a decision-making exercise, a dramatic reading, and the introduction of the "Friends Wheel," students learn why it's difficult to leave abusive relationships and how to help a friend in an abusive relationship.

Learner Outcomes

By the end of this session, students will be able to

- recognize the complexity of the decision to leave an abusive relationship and the many different opinions about when one should leave

- recognize the difficulty and fear that a friend in an abusive relationship may have in reaching out for help

- describe a variety of ways to support a friend who is a victim of dating abuse

- describe the community resources available for teens in abusive dating relationships

- seek help if they're victims of abuse or are abusive partners in a dating relationship

SESSION 4 AT A GLANCE

Total Time: 50 minutes

Part 1: (15 minutes)
Why Don't People Just Leave?

Part 2: (15 minutes)
Why Is It Hard to Get Help?

Part 3: (10 minutes)
How to Help a Friend

Part 4: (8 minutes)
Community Resources

Part 5: (2 minutes)
Conclusion

Materials Needed

☐ ground rules poster (from session 1)

☐ *optional:* student journals (if students didn't keep them)

☐ two pieces of poster board

☐ markers

☐ masking tape

☐ scissors

☐ chalkboard, dry-eraseboard, or flipchart

☐ chalk and/or markers

☐ Friends Wheel ☐ **Handout 11**

☐ Dating Abuse: Who Can Help You? ☐ **Handout 12**

Preparation Needed

1. Read this session's background information.

2. Post the ground rules, if they aren't still up.

3. Cut one piece of poster board in half. On one half, write "I Want to Stay" using a marker. On the other half, write "I Want to Leave." Post the two signs on opposite walls of the classroom. Push furniture to the side so students can easily walk between the two signs.

4. Using a marker, copy the "Friends Wheel" onto the other piece of poster board. Use the Friends Wheel (handout 11) as a template. Copy only the bolded text on the handout onto the poster board. Post the wheel where all students will be able to see it clearly. Also, print and photocopy the handout (one for each student).

5. Find out the names and phone numbers of staff in your school who are equipped to deal with dating abuse situations.

6. Gather information on local community resources that students can turn to if they or a friend are in an abusive relationship or are abusing someone else. For example, include information and phone numbers for your local domestic violence crisis center or hotline, police officers, health department staff, mental health department counselors, hospital emergency rooms, and people at social services.

7. Write or type the information obtained in steps 5 and 6 onto Dating Abuse: Who Can Help You? (handout 12). Photocopy this handout (one for each student).

Background Information

Session 4 begins the *Safe Dates* section on getting help with an abusive relationship. This information is presented in the context of "how to help a friend," so that students who aren't currently involved in an abusive relationship will not tune out.

All students can relate to the need to help friends. In the course of describing how to help friends who are being abused, students who are in abusive relationships themselves will learn how to seek help too.

Adolescents don't typically tell anyone about the abuse in their relationships. When they do confide in someone, it's usually a friend. How friends respond to stories about abuse has a strong influence on how the abused person will feel about the abuse and whether or not she or he will seek help.

Whether or not students have begun dating, they need to develop the skills to help a friend. These skills include understanding the complexity of the situation, not blaming the victim for the abuse, understanding the barriers to seeking help, knowing how to interact with a friend in need, and being familiar with community resources. Information related to each of these skills is discussed during sessions 4 and 5.

SESSION **4** OUTLINE

PART 1
15 minutes

▶ **Why Don't People Just Leave?**

The purpose of part 1 is to address the following questions that are frequently asked of victims in abusive relationships: "Why do you stay? Why don't you just leave?" Asking victims these questions lets them know that their situation is not fully understood. This may cause them to withdraw or make them feel as if they're being blamed for the abuse. To help a friend, one needs to be aware of the complexity of abusive relationships.

1. Explain:

   Today, we're going to discuss how you can help a friend in an abusive relationship. People often turn to friends for help in these situations. To be supportive, you need to understand just how complex abusive relationships can be and how difficult it can be to reach out for help. The first activity asks you to pretend you're in an abusive relationship, and you have to make some difficult choices about staying and trying to "fix" it or leaving.

2. Have the students stand in the middle of the room between the "I Want to Stay" and "I Want to Leave" signs.

3. Explain:

   I'm going to read a story told by a boy named Jose about his girlfriend, Maria. As I read this story, I want each of you to pretend that you are Jose. People often go back and forth in their thinking about a relationship, trying to decide whether to stay or to leave. People also break up and then get back together. Your movements are going to represent Jose's thoughts. When I say something that makes you want to stay in the relationship, stand near the "I Want to Stay" sign. When I say something that makes you want to leave the relationship, stand near the "I Want to Leave" sign.

4. Read the following story to the students. Pause briefly at the end of each action so students have time to move back and forth between the signs.

JOSE'S STORY

I met Maria in high school when I was a freshman. She's hot, and everyone wants to be with her. She's the only one I ever think about. Everyone says I'm so lucky to have her for a girl-friend.   (PAUSE)

So this other girl, Ebony, started flirting with me and told me she liked me. Maria found out and got all up in Ebony's face, and they fought. I guess Maria won because Ebony hasn't even looked at me since then.   (PAUSE)

Maria makes me feel so awesome. She's so popular but she always says that she needs me. I feel like the coolest guy in school.   (PAUSE)

She can be demanding, though. She doesn't want me to even look at other girls.   (PAUSE)

I don't really look at anyone else, but she's always so sure that I'm checking out my other options. She can get pretty jealous. Maria is the hottest girl in school. Why would I even look at other girls?   (PAUSE)

Going out with her is great, though. It feels like we're in our own little world. For my birthday we went to a movie and hung out in the parking lot with a bunch of my friends. It was fun. But after my friends left, it was even better. She gave me a gold chain and told me that she loved me.   (PAUSE)

One day after my birthday, she got really mad when she was try-ing to call me and I didn't answer my cell because it was dead. She said she really needed to talk to me but couldn't get ahold of me. When I asked her what was wrong, she just said it didn't matter anymore. Since then she always wants to know where I'm going, even if I'm just playing basketball with my brothers.

If I go somewhere without telling her, she'll always call or text me on my cell phone constantly and then accuse me of being somewhere I shouldn't be. Usually, she's convinced that I'm out with another girl, even though that's not true.   (PAUSE)

Sometimes when we have these fights, she throws things at me or slaps me. It never hurts.   (PAUSE)

I know that she's just mad because she loves me so much. My parents raised me never to hit a girl, so I just stand there. She has quite a temper.   (PAUSE)

Things are getting worse. Yesterday at the mall, she pinched me because she thought I was looking at another girl.   (PAUSE)

I have pushed her away a couple of times, but it only makes it worse.   (PAUSE)

Every once in a while, I get so frustrated with her mood swings that I try to break up with her. She always comes back crying, "I love you. I need you." She says she's sorry and that she can be a bad girlfriend sometimes, but that if I love her, I'll help her work through these things. Whenever that happens, I remember how cool she can be.   (PAUSE)

The last time I tried to break up, she got embarrassed but explained everything to me, and made me promise not to tell anyone. Her family is really abusive. Her dad hits both her and her mom. She says that she hates him and doesn't want to be like him. Maria doesn't want to hurt me. She would be the perfect girlfriend if she learned to control her temper and stopped getting so jealous. I know she loves me.   (PAUSE)

5. Explain:

    As you can see, abusive relationships can be very complicated. Each of you made different decisions at different points in the story. We all have different priorities.

    Everyone can take a seat now.

6. Ask:

   Those of you who were standing under the "I Want to Stay" sign at the end of Jose's story, why would you remain in a relationship with Maria?

7. List all of the students' responses on the chalkboard, dry-eraseboard, or flipchart.

8. Open up the discussion to everyone in the class. Ask:

   Can anyone else think of other reasons why Jose might want to stay with Maria awhile longer?

   Continue adding ideas to the list.

9. Explain:

   These are all good reasons. There are a lot of reasons that people don't want to leave a relationship, even if it is abusive.

   When you ask a victim of abuse, "Why don't you just leave?" the person may think you're blaming him or her for the abuse. Asking this question shows that you don't completely understand your friend's problem. People stay for many different reasons: because they're in love, because they think the bad parts will go away and the good parts will stay, because they feel responsible for the abuse, because they blame themselves, because they want to help the person, and many more reasons.

   In the rest of this session and in the next session, you will learn more about how to help a friend who is in an abusive dating relationship by showing that you understand how complicated the relationship is, and how to provide him or her with information about how to leave the relationship.

PART 2
15 minutes

▶ **Why Is It Hard to Get Help?**

The purpose of part 2 is to acknowledge the difficulty of seeking help and to describe why people who are victims of abuse often do not seek help. There are three reasons for addressing the barriers to seeking help: (1) so friends understand why a victim of abuse may be hesitant to reach out; (2) so students in abusive relationships feel understood; and (3) so students realize that getting help is difficult for most people in abusive relationships.

1. Explain:

   As you help a friend in an abusive relationship, it's important to understand that reaching out for help is difficult. This may be a time when your friend really needs you. But unless you understand his or her fears, you won't be able to give helpful, supportive advice.

2. Ask:

   Why do you think it might be difficult to tell someone about abuse or violence in a dating relationship?

3. Write students' responses on the chalkboard, dry-eraseboard, or flipchart.

4. Point out the barriers to getting help listed below if the students don't mention them.

Barriers to Getting Help

- fear of hurting their dating partner's feelings
- fear that the friend who they confide in will tell them to end the relationship
- fear of losing independence from one's parents
- fear of getting into trouble with one's parents
- fear that people will not understand, will blame them, or won't believe what's happened
- not knowing how or where to get help
- fear of retaliation from the abusive dating partner
- not knowing how to leave or improve the situation
- embarrassment
- fear of being judged

• not trusting that what is said will be kept confidential

• not wanting to admit that it's a real problem

PART 3
10 minutes

▶ **How to Help a Friend**

The purpose of part 3 is to introduce several important aspects of interacting with a friend who's in an abusive relationship.

1. Explain:

   Now, say that a friend tells you about his or her abusive dating relationship. You understand that he or she must be weighing a lot of options and is confused because he or she cares a lot about his or her dating partner. In addition, you can imagine some of your friend's fears about seeking help. So what do you do?

 Handout 11

2. Point to the Friends Wheel poster. Pass out a copy of the Friends Wheel (handout 11) to each student.

3. Explain:

   The Friends Wheel shows you ways to help a victim of abuse. In the center of the wheel you'll see the phrase "Helping a Friend."

   Teens in abusive relationships are more likely to turn to a friend than an adult or professional. If a friend comes to you upset or in trouble, it's important to be supportive and helpful.

   The Friends Wheel shows six different ways to help a friend in an abusive relationship. Let's think about what each section of this wheel would mean in real life.

4. Ask:

   What do you think is meant by "Don't Gossip"? How could you make your friend feel like you're having a private or confidential conversation?

(Possible answers: your friend should be able to trust you not to spread the news around school, or even to your circle of friends; to confide in you, a friend needs to know his or her story will be kept private)

5. Ask:

What would you say or do in a conversation to show a friend that you "Believe the Story"?

(Possible answers: listen and tell your friend you believe her or him; acknowledge feelings and let your friend know she or he isn't alone)

6. Ask:

What would you say to let a friend know that "He or She Didn't Deserve to Be Abused"?

(Possible answers: tell your friend that he or she did *not* deserve it; the abuse isn't his or her fault; no one deserves to be abused; point out potential negative consequences of the abuse)

7. Ask:

What does it mean to "Let Your Friend Make His or Her Own Decisions"?

(Possible answers: respect your friend's right to make decisions in his or her life, when he or she is ready; acknowledge that your friend is the expert on his or her life)

8. Ask:

What should your friend ask himself or herself when creating a "Safety Plan"?

(Possible answers: what has your friend tried to do in the past to keep safe from the abuse? Is it working? Does she or he have a place to go if an escape is necessary?)

9. Ask:

What are some of the ways that you could "Give Help"?

(Possible answers: know the resources in your community; be a good listener; believe the friend)

10. Explain:

Each of these ways of providing support, encouragement, and respect gives victims of dating abuse strength to deal with their situation.

PART 4
8 minutes

▶ **Community Resources**

The purpose of part 4 is to present the local resources available to teenagers in abusive relationships.

1. Explain:

One of the important ways to help a friend is to connect him or her with professionals who know how to help teens in abusive relationships. These professionals can help your friend think about all of his or her options. In addition, because of their special training, these people can help a victim of abuse develop a safety plan (whether or not he or she wants to remain in the relationship), end the relationship, or protect himself or herself after breaking up with the person.

 Handout 12

2. Give each student a copy of handout 12, Dating Abuse: Who Can Help You?

3. Point out the two national teen dating abuse and date rape hotlines and any local crisis lines that are listed. Emphasize that calls to the national hotlines are confidential, and they do not need to give their name. Find out the confidentiality status of the local hotline (if one is listed) and tell students about it.

Explain:

People in our school, as well as in community organizations, can help teens who are being abused in their dating relationships. You can always go to these people to talk about dating abuse.

Read the names of the people at your school who can help teens.

4. Explain:

Other people in our community are also ready to talk to teens who need help with abusive relationships. These people include . . .

Discuss the contact information provided on this handout.

The following resources address teen dating abuse:

- National Teen Dating Abuse Helpline: 1-866-331-9474
- Rape, Abuse, and Incest National Network (RAINN): 1-800-656-HOPE (4673)
- National Domestic Violence Hotline: 1-800-799-SAFE (7233)
- Break the Cycle: www.breakthecycle.org
- The Safe Space: www.thesafespace.org
- That's Not Cool: www.thatsnotcool.com
- National Youth Violence Prevention Resource Center: www.safeyouth.org

PART 5
2 minutes

▶ **Conclusion**

1. Summarize by saying:

It's important to talk to someone if you're in an abusive relationship. Even though it's hard and sometimes scary to talk about abuse, talking is often the first step to making a change. Whether or not you want to leave a relationship, talking can help you figure out what's happening to you and what decisions you need to make.

In addition to seeking help, it's important to reconnect with your friends and family members. Abuse often isolates victims.

2. *Optional:* Have students add all session 4 handouts to their journals. Remind them to bring their journals to the next session (if you don't collect them).

SESSION 5

Helping Friends

Description

Through stories and role-playing, students practice skills for helping friends who are victims of abuse or confronting friends who are abusive partners.

Learner Outcomes

By the end of this session, students will be able to

- identify red flags that indicate their friend might be an abusive partner or a victim of dating abuse
- feel more comfortable confronting a friend who is abusive in a dating relationship
- understand how to support a friend in an abusive relationship

SESSION 5 AT A GLANCE

Total Time: 50 minutes

Part 1: (8 minutes)
Elijah's Story

Part 2: (8 minutes)
Zoey's Story

Part 3: (30 minutes)
Being a Friend

Part 4: (4 minutes)
Conclusion

Materials Needed

- ☐ ground rules poster (from session 1)
- ☐ *optional:* student journals (if students didn't keep them)
- ☐ Friends Wheel poster (from session 4)
- ☐ Elijah's Story ▯ **Handout 13**
- ☐ Zoey's Story ▯ **Handout 14**
- ☐ pens or pencils
- ☐ Elijah's Statements ▯ **Handout 15**
- ☐ Zoey's Statements ▯ **Handout 16**
- ☐ Guidelines for Helping People Who Are Abusive ▯ **Handout 17**
- ☐ Guidelines for Helping People Who Are Being Abused ▯ **Handout 18**

Preparation Needed

1. Read this session's background information.
2. Post the ground rules, if they aren't still up.
3. Post the Friends Wheel poster, if it isn't still up.
4. Print and photocopy handouts 13–18 (one for each student).

Background Information

In order for students to help friends in abusive situations, they need to be able to identify abuse and feel comfortable talking to their friend about it. This session gives students an opportunity to practice communicating with friends who are victims of abuse or abusive partners.

S E S S I O N **O U T L I N E**

| **PART 1**
8 minutes | ▶ **Elijah's Story** |

▶ **Elijah's Story**

The purpose of parts 1 and 2 is to establish a detailed story of a couple in an abusive relationship that will be referred to throughout the session. During this process, red flags in abusive relationships will be identified.

1. Explain:

   In the last session we talked about empathizing with and helping a friend. Today, we're going to practice the skills we discussed.

2. Point to the Friends Wheel and briefly review the steps in helping a friend who's being abused.

3. Explain:

   I'll need two volunteers—one girl and one boy.

4. Ask the volunteers to come to the front of the classroom but to stand on opposite sides of the room.

🗐 **Handout 13**
🗐 **Handout 14**

5. Give the boy volunteer a copy of Elijah's Story (handout 13). Give the girl volunteer a copy of Zoey's Story (handout 14).

6. Give a copy of Elijah's Story (handout 13) to all the other students.

7. Explain:

   Pretend that Elijah is your friend. As you listen to Elijah telling his story, try to pick out the red flags, or cues, that might let you know he's being abusive. Underline any parts of the story that raise red flags.

8. Have the boy volunteer read Elijah's story out loud.

ELIJAH'S STORY

I started dating Zoey a year ago. She's three years younger than I am. We met at a friend's party. I was sixteen then, and she was thirteen.

Zoey is different from the other girls I've dated. She's very ambitious and her parents encourage her to think about her future a lot. She has great grades in school and wants to be a doctor. Zoey's parents don't allow her to date. I've had to help her get around this so we can see each other. At first she was scared about lying to her parents, but with my help, she's gotten pretty good at it.

Obviously, I'm Zoey's first serious boyfriend. As a result, I have had to teach her a lot about dating. Sometimes she does the stupidest things. She doesn't even think. Like, one day I walked into the lunchroom at school and she was sitting at a table flirting with a bunch of guys! She said they were just friends. What she didn't understand was that things change when you're in a relationship.

She's beautiful and I know what those guys were thinking. She has to start acting more grown-up, like a girlfriend. I grabbed her and pulled her out into the hallway. We had a little talk and I told her that I wouldn't have my girlfriend acting so stupid. She was crying. I didn't mean to leave bruises on her arm or to shout, but she was just acting so immature. I wanted to make sure she understood that it wasn't okay to go around flirting.

Another time she embarrassed me in front of my friends. My friends and I were discussing basketball. I was telling them about a play I had made the previous day. It was an awesome play. Zoey had been there, watching. When I told the story, she laughed a little and told my friends I was exaggerating. I was so embarrassed. I told her she knew nothing about basketball, so she should shut up. She did. When we were alone, I apologized for getting so angry but explained that I couldn't let her embarrass me in front of my friends.

I really do love Zoey. It's hard to date a girl who's so young, though. You have to teach them everything. Zoey looks up to me. She's learning to ask me how things are supposed to be done, rather than acting like such a little girl and just doing whatever.

But yesterday she made me so angry! She said she was going to be home after school, so I went by to see her, knowing both of her parents would be working late. She must have forgotten that she said she'd be home, because she went to a friend's house. She didn't answer her cell phone or respond to any of my texts. I waited for two hours. When Zoey finally got back, I was furious. She seemed surprised, which made me even angrier. I asked her why she didn't answer her cell or text me back. She said that she must have forgotten her cell phone in her locker. When she told me to go home and cool down so we could talk about it calmly, I got so mad that I hit her. The left side of her face is all swollen. I feel really bad, but why can't she learn?

9. Ask:

   What red flags did you find in Elijah's story that indicate he's abusive?

   (Possible answers: the attitude that he should/can teach his girlfriend; insulting her; telling her how to act; forcing her to fit into an image; making her afraid of his anger; intimidating her; making her cry; restricting her behavior; hitting her; leaving bruises)

PART 2
8 minutes

▶ **Zoey's Story**

1. Explain:

   We've heard Elijah's side of the story. Now let's listen to how Zoey sees their relationship.

 Handout 14

2. Give each student a copy of Zoey's Story (handout 14).

Duplicating this page is illegal. Do not copy this material without written permission from the publisher.

87

3. Explain:

Now pretend that you're Zoey's friend. As you listen to Zoey telling her story, try to pick out the red flags, or cues, that might tell you she's being abused. Underline any parts of the story that raise red flags.

4. Ask the girl volunteer to read Zoey's Story.

ZOEY'S STORY

I started dating Elijah about a year ago. He was so sweet when we met. Oh, and he was so romantic. I fell in love with him right away. I was thirteen. He was sixteen. He had just gotten a car for his birthday. We went out on such romantic dates. He'd write the most amazing letters. It was so intense.

My parents don't know about Elijah. Really, I'm not even allowed to date. But Elijah was so persuasive and it felt so good to have someone like me that much. I've had to lie to my parents, though. This hasn't been fun or easy. But Elijah has really helped me out. My parents are clueless. I do feel bad about sneaking around so much. Elijah tells me it's no big deal.

He was the first guy I had ever dated. It was great to have a boyfriend. Everyone seemed to respect me more. He was so strong and could act really tough sometimes. He was always sure that everybody in the school wanted to be with me. He said he was in love and wanted me all to himself. We just couldn't spend enough time together. We just clicked. We were so connected.

People were surprised that Elijah and I hit it off. They said he didn't seem like my type. Elijah does have a temper. When he's in a bad mood, I just try to stay out of his way. It works most of the time. If I can just keep from irritating him, everything is great. The problem is that he gets jealous of everyone.

Sometimes I think he feels like he owns me. When we first started dating, it felt good that he wanted to be with me all of the time, but then it came to mean that I couldn't be with other people, or anyplace without him. When I'm not with him, he calls my cell and texts me almost every two minutes. If I don't answer, he gets really mad. Sometimes I turn my cell off and just tell him the battery died or something.

He doesn't want me talking to any other guys. I have a lot of guy friends. They've been my friends for a long time and I don't want to lose them. I tell Elijah constantly that I love him and he's the only person I want to be with. I try to show him that he's the most important person in the world to me. We've even talked about spending our whole lives together.

Sometimes he can be so tough, and then other times he seems so insecure. Like, one day we were standing in the hall between classes with a bunch of friends. Elijah was bragging about one of his basketball plays. He is so cute, but he can exaggerate. I just giggled a little as he told the story. I suppose that I shouldn't have giggled, but it was really no big deal. Anyway, he shouted at me and told me to shut up. I was so embarrassed and angry. It's as if he wants to show his friends he is in control.

Yesterday was the worst, though. He had yelled at me before, but he had never hit me. I was so shocked. I didn't think he could ever hit me. I know he loves me so much.

Elijah had asked me during school what I was doing in the afternoon, knowing that my parents would be working late. I didn't have any plans, so I said, "Nothing." We didn't make plans or anything. I had no idea that he thought we were going to spend the afternoon together.

So when my friend Carrie called and wanted help dyeing her hair, I went over to her house. Elijah must have come to see me shortly after I left for Carrie's place. He waited until I returned. He was so angry. He asked me why I didn't answer my cell phone or respond to his texts. Actually, my cell was off, but I told him I forgot it in my locker. We never made any plans. I had no idea that he was coming over to my house. He was shouting at me. At first, I didn't even know what he was angry about. Then, he just flew off the handle and hit me across the face.

I don't know how I will explain my bruised and swollen face to my parents.

5. Ask:

   What red flags did you find in Zoey's story that indicate she's being abused?

   (Possible answers: feeling like Elijah's anger is her fault; Elijah's extreme jealousy and feelings of ownership; Elijah's attempts to isolate her, to keep her from her friends; he embarrasses her; yells at her; hits her; expects her to wait around for him)

PART 3
30 minutes

▶ **Being a Friend**

The purpose of part 3 is for students to practice responding to friends who are in abusive dating relationships and to communicate that abuse is not okay and will not be tolerated. If you are short on time, have the students complete only two role-plays for each character instead of three.

1. Explain:

   To put an end to abuse, it's important for the friends and family of both the victim and the abusive partner to let them know that the situation is not okay. Friends of people who are abusive need to take a stand against dating abuse. This action is just as important as supporting someone who is being abused.

2. Have students count off by two. Clear the center of the classroom.

3. Have students who are "1s" pair up with students who are "2s."

4. Explain:

   The 1s are Elijah. The 2s are Elijah's friends. I'm going to give each Elijah a handout with three statements that Elijah will say. The friend's job is to role-play how to respond to an abusive friend who makes such comments.

I'll give each friend a handout about talking to a friend who's abusive. The friends should try to do all of the things on the handout. You'll have four minutes to confront Elijah about his behavior after he makes his statement.

After four minutes, I'm going to yell, "Switch!" and all the 1s should pair up with a new 2. Then each Elijah should be facing a new friend. The new friend will say, "Hi!" Elijah will make his second statement, and the role-play will begin with the new friend's response.

Then we'll switch pairs one more time. Elijah will make his third statement and the role-play will begin with the new friend's response. After each person does three role-plays based on Elijah's scenario, the 2s will become Zoey and the 1s will become Zoey's friend. The same procedure will occur, except Zoey will be making the statement, and Zoey's friend must address the issue of dating abuse with a victim.

□ **Handout 15**

□ **Handout 17**

5. Pass out handout 15, Elijah's Statements, to the 1s. Give the 2s a copy of handout 17, Guidelines for Helping People Who Are Abusive.

6. Briefly go over the Guidelines for Helping People Who Are Abusive handout. Then have the class do Elijah's role-plays.

□ **Handout 16**

□ **Handout 18**

7. When Elijah's role-plays are done, give the 2s a copy of handout 16, Zoey's Statements. Give the 1s a copy of handout 18, Guidelines for Helping People Who Are Being Abused.

8. Briefly go over the Guidelines for Helping People Who Are Being Abused handout. Then have the class do Zoey's role-plays.

9. After the three role-plays with Zoey have been completed, ask everyone to return to their seats.

10. Pass out additional handouts, so everyone has a copy of Guidelines for Helping People Who Are Abusive and Guidelines for Helping People Who Are Being Abused.

    Optional: Have students keep these guidelines in their journals.

11. Ask students to reflect on this experience of confronting a friend. Ask:

    Was it easy? Was it difficult? Do you think it would be easy or difficult in real life?

PART 4
4 minutes

▶ **Conclusion**

1. Explain:

   It's often difficult to talk to friends about dating abuse. There are a lot of attitudes, stereotypes, and mixed emotions that surround the topic. However, if we want to stop the abuse in our lives, school, and community, we have to take a stand against it. It's important to tell people who are abusive that their behavior is not okay, and it's important to support people who are being abused.

   We all see abuse too often—at home, between friends, on television, and so on—and we may begin to see it as "normal." We need to remind each other that abuse isn't normal and we all deserve happy, healthy, and fun relationships.

2. *Optional:* Have students add all session 5 handouts to their journals. Remind them to bring their journals to the next session (if you don't collect them).

SESSION 6

Overcoming Gender Stereotypes

Description

Through a writing exercise, small-group discussion, and scenarios, students learn about gender stereotypes and how these stereotypes can affect dating relationships.

Learner Outcomes

By the end of this session, students will be able to

- understand that they and other people hold specific images of dating relationships

- describe how the images people hold influence their interactions in a dating relationship

- identify the harmful consequences of gender stereotyping

- explain the role that gender stereotyping plays in dating relationships

SESSION 6 AT A GLANCE

Total Time: 50 minutes

Part 1: (3 minutes)
Introduction

Part 2: (7 minutes)
Unfair Expectations

Part 3: (5 minutes)
Images and Where They Come From

Part 4: (10 minutes)
Associations

Part 5: (13 minutes)
Gender Stereotypes

Part 6: (10 minutes)
Stereotyping Leads to Abuse

Part 7: (2 minutes)
Conclusion

Duplicating this page is illegal. Do not copy this material without written permission from the publisher.

93

Materials Needed

- ☐ ground rules poster (from session 1)
- ☐ *optional:* student journals (if students didn't keep them)
- ☐ blank paper
- ☐ pens or pencils
- ☐ chalkboard, dry-eraseboard, or flipchart
- ☐ chalk or markers
- ☐ Stereotypes and Dating Abuse Scenarios 🖉 **Handout 19**

Preparation Needed

1. Read this session's background information.
2. Post the ground rules, if they aren't still up.
3. Print and photocopy handout 19 (one for each student).

Background Information

Session 6 may be a more challenging session to facilitate because each of us holds our own stereotypes. These can blind us to similar stereotypes in others. As you facilitate the discussion in this session, it's important to recognize your own biases.

To ensure that this session doesn't simply acknowledge and reinforce gender stereotypes, point out the negative consequences of gender stereotyping several times. Emphasize the link between gender stereotyping and dating abuse. There are three ways in which gender stereotyping may lead to abuse:

1. Stereotypes may support abusive behavior (such as "women should be submissive to men").
2. Stereotypes people hold of their own gender may encourage them to use abuse (such as "men have to act tough").
3. Stereotypes people hold of their partner's gender may give them reason to be abusive (for example, a young woman becomes angry and abusive with her boyfriend because he isn't rich enough, tough enough, or athletic enough).

Some of the students in your class may come from countries or be of religions that hold traditional gender stereotypes about men and women. Be sensitive to these students' perspectives, while still pointing out the harmful aspects of gender stereotyping for both men and women.

Duplicating this page is illegal. Do not copy this material without written permission from the publisher.

95

SESSION 6 OUTLINE

PART 1
3 minutes

▶ **Introduction**

1. Explain:

   In the last five sessions we've been talking about dating abuse. As a class, we've discussed what types of actions are abusive and why people act in abusive ways. We've also discussed how to help a friend who is either the victim of dating abuse or the abusive partner.

   During the next four sessions, we're going to talk about how to prevent dating abuse. The information and skills we'll be working on are very important in dating relationships. This information is helpful for people who have not yet begun dating, as well as for those who are dating now.

   We'll be talking about

   • **gender stereotypes in dating relationships**

   • **communication skills**

   • **positive ways to respond to anger and jealousy**

   • **how to prevent dating sexual abuse**

PART 2
7 minutes

▶ **Unfair Expectations**

The purpose of part 2 is to help students see how they've personally experienced unfair expectations from others so they can better relate to the abstract concept of gender stereotyping.

1. Explain:

   It's normal to hold expectations of ourselves, of other people, and of relationships. Sometimes, however, such expectations seem unfair. Perhaps a father expects his son to be the best football player in the school. Or a boyfriend expects his girlfriend to wait by the phone every night for his call. Unfair expectations can make you angry, sad, insecure, and frustrated.

2. Explain:

   Take a moment to think about the last time someone held an unfair expectation of you.

   Give students a minute to think about a situation in their own lives.

3. Explain:

   Now, I'd like you to take out a piece of paper and briefly write about the last time someone held an unfair expectation of you.

   Hand out paper and pens or pencils, if students don't have these supplies. Give students only a few minutes to write what happened.

4. Then ask the class if anyone would like to share his or her experience. Allow a few students to share.

5. Explain:

   As we talk about today's topic, remember the feelings you had when someone held unfair expectations of you.

PART 3
5 minutes

▶ **Images and Where They Come From**

The purpose of part 3 is to help students understand that we have images of how people should act in relationships and that these images are created by and transmitted throughout our society in many different ways.

1. Explain:

   The expectations people hold of you come from images they have of who they want you to be or how they want you to act. People hold images of many different kinds of relationships. Today, we're going to talk about dating relationships, but a lot of what we talk about applies to other relationships as well.

We all have images of what dating relationships are supposed to be like. They're like scripts that we follow when we're dating someone. These images, or scripts, are very important because they influence how you treat someone you're dating and how your boyfriend or girlfriend treats you.

2. Ask:

    Where do you think most teens get their images of what dating relationships should be like?

    Write all of the students' answers on the chalkboard, dry-eraseboard, or flipchart.

    (Possible answers: television; song lyrics; music videos; magazines; books; advertising; movies; family members [parents, sisters, brothers, and so on]; peers; community organizations [such as churches and synagogues]; role models [both positive and negative]; teachers)

PART 4
10 minutes

▶ **Associations**

The purpose of part 4 is to show students that they hold certain images about people, and to draw out some of the stereotypes in our society.

1. Explain:

    Because we constantly get messages from these different places (point to the list just developed by the students), **sometimes we have certain expectations about people and relationships without even realizing it. We just hear or see things so often that they stick in our minds. This next exercise will help identify some of the expectations you may hold.**

2. Ask for a volunteer to help you demonstrate the next exercise.

3. Explain:

    During this exercise, you'll work in pairs. One person will say a word that refers to the gender that is different than that of the other person in your pair. For example, if my partner is a male, I'm going to use words that refer to females (such as woman, girl, mom). As the first person calls out a word, the second person simply says the first thing that pops into his or her head. This is called free association.

4. Demonstrate the process with the volunteer.

    Here's an example of how the exercise might work:

FIRST PERSON	SECOND PERSON
male	strong
boy	show-off
man	rich
guy	cute
father	stern
boyfriend	romantic

5. Have students work in pairs. After one partner has had a chance to free-associate, have the partners switch roles.

6. After all of the students have played both roles, explain:

    This exercise often brings up "gender stereotypes" that we hold. Gender stereotypes are generalizations, mental pictures, and beliefs about what all men and women are like.

    Sometimes the first thing that pops into a person's head is something that the person may not even agree with. For example, someone says "guy" and the partner responds by saying "tough." We know that not all guys are tough; however, in our society guys are often portrayed this way. Many people expect guys to be tough.

Duplicating this page is illegal. Do not copy this material without written permission from the publisher.

99

Gender stereotypes aren't necessarily negative characteristics. An issue is that stereotypes can box people into
a specific way of acting because they're men or because
they're women, rather than allowing them to be individuals.

7. Use examples from your demonstration (step 4 above) to
point out gender stereotypes.

PART 5
13 minutes

▶ **Gender Stereotypes**

The purpose of part 5 is to help students understand how gender
stereotypes affect interactions in a dating relationship. Gender
stereotypes create expectations that are referred to as "dating
stereotypes."

Teacher's Tip ✓

You may have to probe
students during this
exercise. At first the
answers may seem
the same, but ask
students directly, "Is
it the same for girls
and boys?" or "What's
different for girls and
boys?" The differences
may be subtle, but it's
important to draw out
these distinctions.

1. Explain:

**The gender stereotypes that we knowingly or unknowingly
hold affect the way we think about interactions between
men and women. As a result, we create expectations about
the way boyfriends and girlfriends should act.**

**I'm going to give you some scenarios. Then I'm going to
ask a couple of questions about how a boy would act and
how a girl would act in each circumstance.**

2. Read the following scenarios out loud:

Scenario 1: Chris likes Alex and wants to go out on a date.

Chris is a boy and Alex is a girl. What does Chris do?

Chris is a girl and Alex is a boy. What does Chris do?

(Possible stereotypes: only boys can ask girls out; girls must
wait for boys to ask them out; boys should pursue girls; girls
should play "hard to get")

Scenario 2: Chris and Alex have been dating for two months. Chris finds out Alex is seeing someone else.

Chris is a girl. What does she do?

Chris is a boy. What does he do?

(Possible stereotypes: girls cry and get upset; boys get mad and violent; boys cannot commit; girls are "fickle"; "boys will be boys"; girls try to win back their boyfriends)

Scenario 3: Chris and Alex go on a date to the movies.

Who pays for the movie? Why?

(Possible stereotypes: boys pay for a date; girls "owe" the boy something if he pays for the date; if a girl pays, she'll make the boy feel inadequate)

Scenario 4: Chris and Alex go to Chris's house at the end of the date.

Chris is a boy. What does he do?

Chris is a girl. What does she do?

(Possible stereotypes: the boy makes physical advances; the girl resists those advances)

3. Ask:

    Why do you think people use stereotypes?

    (Possible answers: because it's easier to think about people that way; because people are afraid of others they don't understand or know; pressure from society to do so)

4. Ask:

    How can stereotypes hurt people?

    (Possible answers: stereotypes influence how people act; they blame people when they're innocent; they don't allow people to be seen as individuals; they limit relationships)

5. Ask:

How do you feel about dating stereotypes? Do you agree with them? Do you follow them? Why or why not?

6. Explain:

We each have the right to decide how we treat others and how we want to be treated by others. We have the right to these decisions even if they don't fit into the mold made by gender and dating stereotypes.

PART 6
10 minutes

▶ **Stereotyping Leads to Abuse**

The purpose of part 6 is to highlight the link between stereotypical beliefs and abusive behavior.

1. Explain:

Sometimes gender stereotyping may lead to abuse.

Handout 19

2. Give each student a copy of handout 19, Stereotypes and Dating Abuse Scenarios.

3. Explain:

I'm going to read two scenarios that we talked about in session 2. This time, however, I want you to think about the scenarios in terms of gender stereotyping.

Teacher's Tip ✓

The scenario indicates that abuse is a regular part of Jason and Megan's relationship. Megan may hold a stereotype that all men are violent.

4. Read the following scenario from handout 19 out loud to the class:

Jason invited several of his friends and his girlfriend, Megan, to his house to watch movies on Friday night. Jason asked Megan if she would put out some chips and drinks for everyone. She said that she didn't mind. When Jason's friends arrived, they all sat down to watch movies.

When someone finished a drink or when the bowl of chips was empty, Jason would tell Megan to go to the kitchen for refills. When this happened for the third time, Megan said

that she wouldn't be their waitress. She wanted to watch the movie and they could help themselves to the food in the kitchen if they wanted it.

Jason got angry. He ordered Megan to get his friends' drinks. When she refused, Jason hit her across the face and pulled her into the kitchen. Jason's friends had seen Jason and Megan fight like this many times.

Teacher's Tip ✓

The scenario indicates that Jason's friends had seen him acting abusively toward Megan many times. They may accept this without interfering because they hold stereotypes that make them think Megan should wait on Jason and them, or they may think that Jason needs to take control.

5. Use the following questions to facilitate a discussion about how gender stereotypes led to the abuse in this scenario:

   a. **What stereotypes does Jason hold of females?**

      (Possible answers: women should be hostesses; women should be caretakers; women should do work in the kitchen; women should always listen to and obey men)

   b. **What stereotypes does Jason hold of males?**

      (Possible answers: men should be in control; men should give the orders; men should be waited on; men should be taken care of)

   c. **Did Megan hold any stereotypes?**

      (Possible answer: all men are violent)

   d. **Did Jason's friends hold any stereotypes?**

      (Possible answers: women should wait on men; the man needs to take control)

6. Explain:

   Jason has an image of how Megan is supposed to act based on gender stereotypes. When she doesn't act this way, he is abusive. Would Jason have acted this way toward a male friend?

7. Read the following scenario from handout 19 out loud to the class:

   Tyrone bought Nicole an iTunes gift card for her birthday so she could buy new music for her iPod. Nicole opened the gift card and at first she seemed to love the gift. Then, however, she asked where the rest of her gifts were. When Tyrone said that he just got the iTunes gift card for her birthday present, Nicole got angry. She started screaming at him. She said that she expected more than a stupid gift card for her birthday, and she threw the gift card across the room.

8. Use the following questions to facilitate a discussion about how gender stereotypes led to the abuse in the scenario above:

   a. **What stereotypes does Nicole hold of males?**

      (Possible answers: men should be rich; men should provide for their girlfriends [wives, and so on]; men should financially support the women in their lives; men show love by giving things to women)

   b. **What stereotypes does Nicole hold of females?**

      (Possible answers: women need to be financially supported; women get what they want by being emotional and abusive)

   c. **Did Tyrone hold any stereotypes?**

      (Possible answer: women are emotional, irrational, and/or demanding, so this type of behavior is normal)

Teacher's Tip ✓

Tyrone's stereotypes weren't demonstrated directly in the scenario, but the students might speculate what they are.

9. *Optional:* Ask students to share any gender stereotypes they've run into in dating relationships or in friendships with the opposite sex. Be sure teens don't use names or too many details out of respect for others.

PART 7
2 minutes

▶ **Conclusion**

1. Explain:

   Television, movies, song lyrics, parents, and friends reflect how people are "supposed to" act in our society. Some

of these stereotypes are positive and some are negative. Gender stereotypes provide images of females and males.

If your dating partner or you feel as if you have to live up to these images, then there may be conflict, disappointment, and frustration. If you're aware of the messages being sent to you, however, then you can choose to accept or reject them. You can design your own relationships with your partners. You can set up a relationship that fits your personal beliefs about how you want to be treated and how you want to treat others.

When you're in a relationship, think about your expectations for your dating partner. Are they reasonable and fair, or are your expectations based on gender stereotypes?

2. *Optional:* Have students add the session 6 handout to their journals. Remind them to bring their journals to the next session (if you don't collect them).

SESSION 7

How We Feel, How We Deal

Description

Through the use of a feelings diary and a discussion of "hot buttons," students learn how to recognize and effectively handle their anger, so it doesn't lead to abusive behavior.

Learner Outcomes

By the end of this session, students will be able to

- express their feelings or emotions in various ways
- understand the importance of acknowledging and communicating their feelings
- identify situations that trigger their anger
- identify physiological and psychological cues that they're angry
- identify a variety of nonviolent ways to respond to anger
- understand that they have a choice in how to respond to anger
- increasingly use nonviolent responses to anger

**SESSION 7
AT A GLANCE**

Total Time: 50 minutes

Part 1: (6 minutes)
Extending Your
Feeling Vocabulary

Part 2: (12 minutes)
Hot Buttons

Part 3: (10 minutes)
Knowing When
You're Angry

Part 4: (7 minutes)
Calming Strategies

Part 5: (12 minutes)
Dealing with Anger

Part 6: (3 minutes)
Conclusion

Materials Needed

☐ ground rules poster (from session 1)

☐ *optional:* student journals (if students didn't keep them)

☐ chalkboard, dry-eraseboard, or flipchart

☐ chalk or a marker

☐ Hot Buttons ☐ **Handout 20**

☐ Feelings ☐ **Handout 21**

☐ Feelings Diary ☐ **Handout 22**

☐ pens or pencils

☐ blank notepaper

Preparation Needed

1. Read this session's background information.

2. Post the ground rules, if they aren't still up.

3. Print and photocopy handouts 20–22 (one for each student).

Background Information

Uncontrollable anger is often used as a reason for dating abuse. Session 7 emphasizes that a person's response to anger is a choice. During this session, not only will (potential) abusive partners practice skills for dealing with anger nonviolently but also (potential) victims of abuse will see that anger isn't an excuse for violent behavior.

S E S S I O N ⑦ O U T L I N E

PART 1
6 minutes

▶ **Extending Your Feeling Vocabulary**

The purpose of part 1 is to encourage students to think about their feelings, to recognize different types of feelings, and to acknowledge the importance of feelings.

1. Explain:

   Today, we're going to talk about the feelings that you have and how you deal with your feelings. All feelings are important. Too often people ignore their feelings or think that their feelings are bad. But feelings can tell you when something is wrong or right. They can also let you know if you need to make changes about a situation.

   When dating, or when you start dating, you'll feel a lot of different emotions. You may feel different things at the same time or your feelings may change quickly. It's important to recognize all your feelings. Too often people get trapped into thinking that there are only three primary feelings: mad, sad, and happy.

2. Ask:

   What are other feelings that people have besides mad, sad, and happy?

   List all responses on the board.

3. Explain:

   It's good to have a big "feeling vocabulary." If you recognize your feelings, you can better understand yourself and you can make yourself better understood by others.

   All feelings are important. They often tell us about a situation, even before our brains can process anything. We can't change our feelings, but we can learn skills to deal with our feelings.

Anger is one feeling we have sometimes. You'll probably feel angry toward your girlfriend or boyfriend at some point. It's all right to be angry. How you deal with that anger, though, can make the difference between a healthy and unhealthy relationship. For the remainder of this session, we're going to talk about dealing with anger.

PART 2
12 minutes

▶ **Hot Buttons**

The purpose of part 2 is to acknowledge that everyone has things that "set him or her off." By helping students identify what personally makes them angry, they'll walk away from this session with a list of times to catch themselves. If people know what triggers their anger, they may feel as if they have more control over it.

1. Explain:

   Everyone has "hot buttons." Hot buttons are those things that make you angry whenever you feel, see, or hear them. Hot buttons are things that irritate you, "get under your skin," or in other ways make you angry.

2. Give students an example of one of your hot buttons and some other examples as well, so they understand the concept.

   (Possible answers: someone who's always late; someone who doesn't follow through on promises; someone being loud and obnoxious; situations where you feel out of control; situations where you don't think you're being heard; when someone does something that hurts your feelings)

3. Explain:

   Take a minute to think about what your hot buttons are.

   Give students a minute or two to sit quietly and think about their hot buttons.

📋 **Handout 20**

4. Give each student a copy of handout 20, Hot Buttons.

5. Explain:

   List a few of your personal hot buttons on the top half of the handout.

6. Give the students a minute or two to write down some of their hot buttons.

7. Ask the students if they'd like to share some of their hot buttons. Allow a few students to respond.

8. Explain:

   If you recognize your hot buttons, you'll be better prepared to control your anger.

PART 3
10 minutes

▶ **Knowing When You're Angry**

The purpose of part 3 is to help students focus on the feeling of getting angry. If they can identify when their anger is building, they'll have time to come up with an appropriate response, rather than blindly exploding in rage.

1. Explain:

   Hot buttons cause us to be angry. Sometimes, however, we don't realize how angry we are until we're about to explode. If you're going to control your anger and use it in positive ways, then you have to realize when a hot button has been pushed. Our bodies give us cues when we're angry. Some of the cues are physical and some are psychological.

2. Explain:

   Think about times when you've been angry. There are two different kinds of anger: immediate anger and pent-up anger. Sometimes people get angry about something specific. A hot button is pushed and right away they're angry. This is immediate anger. At other times, little things build up. The anger seems to grow over time until you

Teacher's Tip ✓

You'll need to probe students and focus them on immediate reactions. Most people don't know their immediate reactions to anger. They see themselves as being calm, something happens, and then they're angry.

Teacher's Tip ✓

This exercise asks students to go through their physiological and psychological reactions that make them aware of their anger. Yelling, hitting, and talking are not a person's first response to anger. You may have to ask students to continually back up to before the incident and to think about how they felt. Ask them to concentrate on their body's response.

feel like you are going to explode—and sometimes you do explode. This is pent-up anger.

First, think about times when you get angry quickly at a specific action or comment. When this happens, what are some cues that let you know you're angry? Write these cues on the Hot Buttons handout under "Immediate Anger."

Some Responses to Immediate Anger

- clenching fists
- grinding teeth
- sweaty palms
- increased heart rate
- tensing muscles
- glaring
- scowling
- change in arm and body position

- chills, shudders, goose bumps
- headache
- red face
- get very quiet
- watering eyes
- hard to swallow
- "butterflies" in the stomach

3. Ask the class if anyone would like to share some of the ways they know they're angry. Allow several students to share.

4. Explain:

Sometimes anger builds over a long time: days, weeks, months, even years. Instead of letting these feelings of anger out, you keep them bottled up and the anger starts to build, until you can no longer contain the anger and you just explode. When this happens, what are some cues that let you know you're angry, or letting anger build up? Write these cues on the Hot Buttons handout under "Pent-Up Anger."

Some Responses to Pent-Up Anger

- fantasize about telling someone off
- start resenting the person
- start making nasty comments about the person
- withdraw from the person
- find yourself obsessing over the situation

This list is often difficult to make. If anger is "pent up," people tend to deny it. They may not even recognize their feelings as anger.

5. Ask the class if anyone would like to share some of the ways they know they're angry. Allow several students to respond.

6. Explain:

If you can identify your own physical or psychological cues to anger, you'll be able to deal with that anger, rather than just feeling out of control.

PART 4
7 minutes

▶ **Calming Strategies**

The purpose of part 4 is to demonstrate that anger is controllable. People choose their actions when they're angry. They can choose to be abusive or to not be abusive.

1. Explain:

Many teenagers who have been abusive to their dating partner claim that they were so angry, it was uncontrollable. They were seeing red. They couldn't stop themselves. When this so-called uncontrollable anger was gone, they were sorry.

Anger, however, is never uncontrollable. We make a choice about how we respond to anger.

2. Explain:

In the few seconds after you realize a hot button has been pushed, your thinking is clear and you can make a choice about how you are going to respond to the anger. But you may only have a few seconds, so you need to have in mind some immediate calming strategies you can use before you get really angry. One example is taking a deep breath. It is also good to think about things you can do later to help you calm down. One example is to go for a walk.

3. Ask:

What are some immediate calming strategies that you can use in the few seconds after your hot button is pushed, but when your thinking is still clear?

Write all of the students' suggestions on the board.

Examples of Immediate Calming Strategies

- take a deep breath
- talk to myself (positive self-talk like "stay cool," "relax," "take it easy")
- cry
- go into another room for a few minutes
- think of something that makes me happy
- tell the person why I am angry
- go into another room and scream
- walk away
- use humor (tell a joke)
- count forward or backward

4. Ask:

What are some later calming strategies that you can use to calm down?

Write all of the students' suggestions on the board.

Examples of Later Calming Strategies

- go for a walk/run

- exercise strenuously

- ask someone for advice

- explain to the person why I'm angry

- listen to music

- play cards, like solitaire

- take a nap

- go dancing

- watch a movie

- clean my room

- play a sport

- read a book

- call a friend

5. Say:

On handout 20, Hot Buttons, write down three immediate calming strategies and three later calming strategies that you would prefer to use.

6. Explain:

Anger can be a positive thing if you handle it carefully. If you don't, it's likely to explode and hurt people. Anger can tell us a lot about a situation. It can be a warning sign that we're in a situation we need to change. Therefore, denying that we're angry is not good. If we're angry, we need to acknowledge the feeling and let others know that we don't support or enjoy the current situation. The important thing is to do this in a positive way.

PART 5
12 minutes

▶ **Dealing with Anger**

The purpose of part 5 is to give students a chance to think about how they want to deal with anger and to outline options for themselves.

1. Explain:

   Now that you've thought about your hot buttons, how you know when you're angry, and calming strategies you can use, it's time to think about how you want to respond the next time you're angry.

2. Give each student a blank piece of notepaper (if they don't have their own).

3. Explain:

   Think about a time when you were angry—a time you wouldn't mind sharing with other people. Write a description of what made you angry (the hot button), how you knew you were angry (immediate or pent-up response), and what you did as a result of that anger.

4. Give the students a few minutes to write down the situation in which they were angry.

5. Divide the class into pairs.

6. Explain:

   Tell your partner about the situation that made you angry and what you did as a result. Together, come up with a list of positive, nonviolent ways that you could have responded to that situation, including immediate and later calming strategies. Write down the possible responses and circle the one you like the best.

   Each partner will have five minutes to tell his or her story and to think about other ways of responding. When the time is up for the first person, I'll yell "Switch" and it will be the second person's turn to tell his or her story and to think about other possible responses to the situation.

Teacher's Tip ✓

If students choose a solution that involves ignoring or stuffing their anger, remind them that you want them to honestly confront the situation.

7. Give the first person five minutes; then say "Switch."

8. Give the second person five minutes too.

9. Remind the students to circle the solution they like the best. Give them a minute to do this if they didn't do it in their pairs.

10. *Optional:* Have a couple of pairs share the solutions they chose.

PART 6
3 minutes

▶ **Conclusion**

1. Explain:

    Anger is controllable. You choose the actions you take when you're angry. You can teach yourself to do things that reduce your anger without hurting others. Controlling your anger is easier when you recognize what makes you angry (your hot buttons), when you can identify your own physical and psychological cues to anger, and when you have calming strategies in mind for dealing with anger.

 Handout 21
Handout 22

2. Give each student a copy of handout 21, Feelings, and handout 22, Feelings Diary.

3. Explain:

    Recognizing your feelings is an important part of dealing with your anger. For homework, I want you to work on identifying your feelings. On the first handout is a list of feeling words. The second handout is a "Feelings Diary."

    From the time you leave class today until you go to bed tonight, keep track of all the different feelings you have and write them down in your Feelings Diary. You can use the feelings vocabulary list to help you think of the appropriate words. You can use your own words too. I will be checking to make sure you did this homework assignment during our next session, but I won't look

at what you wrote. This is a private exercise, for your eyes only.

4. *Optional:* Have students put all their session 7 handouts in their journals. Remind them to bring their journals to the next session (if you don't collect them).

SESSION 8

Equal Power through Communication

Description

Students learn the four SAFE skills for effective communication and practice these skills in a variety of role-plays.

Learner Outcomes

By the end of this session, students will be able to

- describe the four SAFE communication skills for resolving conflict

- demonstrate the use of the four SAFE communication skills

- describe some nonviolent responses when a dating partner doesn't communicate in a way that is fair and equal

**SESSION 8
AT A GLANCE**

Total Time: 50 minutes

Part 1: (5 minutes)
The Four SAFE
Skills for Effective
Communication

Part 2: (15 minutes)
Identifying
Communication Skills

Part 3: (20 minutes)
Role-Playing
Communication Skills

Part 4: (8 minutes)
What If It
Doesn't Work?

Part 5: (2 minutes)
Conclusion

Materials Needed

- [ ] ground rules poster (from session 1)
- [ ] *optional:* student journals (if students didn't keep them)
- [ ] Four SAFE Skills for Building Equal Power through Communication **Handout 23**
- [ ] LaToya and Marcus Script **Handout 24A**
- [ ] two chairs
- [ ] LaToya and Marcus Checklist **Handout 24B**
- [ ] Conflict Situation 1 and Conflict Skills Checklist 1 **Handouts 25A and 25B**
- [ ] Conflict Situation 2 and Conflict Skills Checklist 2 **Handouts 26A and 26B**
- [ ] Conflict Situation 3 and Conflict Skills Checklist 3 **Handouts 27A and 27B**

Preparation Needed

1. Read this session's background information.
2. Post the ground rules, if they aren't still up.
3. Print and photocopy handouts 23–27 (one for each student).

Background Information

The purpose of session 8 is to give students a framework for positive, open communication and to give them an opportunity to practice using this framework. As a result, this session involves a lot of moving around and small-group activity.

You should expect the classroom to be noisy at times. If you move around the room during small-group activities and are available to answer individual questions, this will help groups focus and keep on task.

The message that students take away with them should be that conflict exists and will always exist in relationships. However, if we choose our words carefully, we can avoid attacking or abusing other people.

The *Safe Dates* communication steps are a concrete example of how to communicate openly without always giving in to or attempting to control the other person. Effective communication allows both people to feel powerful in the relationship.

As students enter the room, check with them to make sure they completed their Feelings Diary from session 7. Don't ask to see the feelings they wrote down, just check to make sure the handout was completed.

PART 1
5 minutes

▶ **The Four SAFE Skills for Effective Communication**

The purpose of part 1 is to introduce and explain some fundamental communication skills. The *Safe Dates* model includes four different skills of open communication. Communication is presented as a method through which people in a relationship can both have equal power.

1. Explain:

   Effective communication is important in all parts of our lives. In dating relationships, open and honest communication is essential. Today, we're going to talk about positive ways to communicate with your boyfriend or girlfriend. If you're having an argument with your boyfriend or girlfriend, positive communication skills can help you work through the situation without being hurtful or abusive.

🖰 **Handout 23**

2. Give each student a copy of handout 23, Four SAFE Skills for Building Equal Power through Communication.

3. Explain:

   Here are four basic communication skills that can help you resolve conflict effectively. Each skill is represented by one letter in the word "SAFE."

4. Going down the list of communication skills, ask the students:

   What do you think *(each skill)* means? Clarify or refine the students' responses according to the information given under each skill on the following page.

Four SAFE Skills for Building Equal Power through Communication

Stay calm.

- Use calming strategies to feel cool and collected.

Ask questions.

- Ask honest and open questions to better understand the situation.
- Don't jump to conclusions.
- After listening to your dating partner's answers, you may realize that the conflict was all a misunderstanding.

Find out feelings.

- Find out how the other person feels about the situation that is causing the disagreement.
- Express your own feelings—be honest and specific, referring to the situation and what about it upsets you.
- Use "I statements" when expressing your feelings. Say, "I feel (add a feeling here) when you (add the behavior you don't like here) because (add your reason for feeling like you do here)." (For example, "I feel mad when you ignore me because I feel like you don't care.")

Exchange ideas for a possible solution.

- With all of this information, suggest possible solutions.
- Talk about which ones work best for the two of you.

5. Explain:

   These communication skills are useful in establishing new relationships or in ongoing, healthy relationships where both people feel secure. In a relationship where power isn't shared equally and/or abuse is going on, these skills may not be useful on their own. Teens in these situations should seek outside help from one of the resources discussed in session 4.

6. *Optional:* Make more copies of the Four SAFE Skills for Building Equal Power through Communication handout. Laminate them and post them in your classroom or around your school.

PART 2
15 minutes

▶ **Identifying Communication Skills**

The purpose of part 2 is to give students a chance to identify these communication skills in a realistic situation.

1. Explain:

   Now we're going to try to pick out these communication skills in a conversation between LaToya and Marcus.

🖕 **Handout 24A**

2. Give each student a copy of handout 24A, LaToya and Marcus Script.

3. Ask for two volunteers to act out the scenario in front of the class. One volunteer will read LaToya's part and the other will read Marcus's part. Set two chairs in front of the room.

4. Explain:

   As the role-play is being acted out, listen for each of the four SAFE skills of communication.

5. Have a student read the background information on the handout out loud.

6. Instruct the two volunteers to act out the rest of the role-play as described on the handout.

🖕 **Handout 24B**

7. Pass out a copy of handout 24B, LaToya and Marcus Checklist, to each student.

8. Explain:

   Now that you've heard LaToya and Marcus's conversation, try to identify the four SAFE communication skills they used. You can go back through the script if needed. First go down the column labeled LaToya, and mark an "X" next to each communication skill she used. Then go down the column labeled Marcus, and mark an "X" next to each communication skill he used.

9. Give the students a few minutes to complete this task.

10. When the students are done, ask them which communication skills LaToya used and how she used them.

11. Then ask students which communication skills Marcus used and how he used them.

PART 3
20 minutes

▶ **Role-Playing Communication Skills**

The purpose of part 3 is to have students practice using the four SAFE communication skills.

1. Explain:

   Communication is a skill. No one is a born communicator, but everyone can learn to assert himself or herself while respecting the feelings and beliefs of others. In the next exercise, we're all going to practice the four SAFE communication skills.

2. Explain:

   First, I'm going to divide the class into groups of three. Each group will have to choose a recorder, someone to be student A, and someone to be student B. Everyone will have a chance to play all three roles. You just need to choose who's going to perform each role first.

   After you're in groups, I'll pass out descriptions of the characters. These descriptions will tell you how your character feels and what she or he thinks about the situation. You should use the information in these descriptions to have a conversation with your partner. The goal of this conversation is for each person to use all of the SAFE communication skills.

   The recorder will watch the conversation and mark down how many skills each person uses.

3. Divide the students into groups of three. Have each group decide who's going to be the recorder the first time. The recorder will rotate for each of the three conflicts to be acted out so everyone will record one time.

Handout 25B

4. Pass out handout 25B, Conflict Skills Checklist 1, to the recorder in each group. Describe the role of the recorder:

   The recorder must listen very carefully to the discussion being acted out in front of him or her. Watch for the four SAFE communication skills. Put a check under the name of the appropriate person when he or she demonstrates one of the skills.

5. Have each group decide who is going to be student A and who will be student B.

Handout 25A

6. Pass out handout 25A, Conflict Situation 1, role-play descriptions to the students. Ask them to read the descriptions silently without sharing with the other people in their group. For both actors, the goal is to use as many of the four SAFE communication skills as possible.

   Introduce conflict 1 as follows:

   The two people in the first role-play should pretend to be texting on their cell phones. Keshia has just sent a text to Liam and is waiting for him to text her back. She asked him what time he's coming to pick her up. Begin your role-play.

7. After a few minutes, ask the students to switch roles so there is a new recorder, a new student A, and a new student B.

Handout 26A
Handout 26B

8. Pass out handout 26A, Conflict Situation 2, role-play descriptions and handout 26B, Conflict Skills Checklist 2, recorder's sheet.

9. Ask students to read the descriptions silently.

10. Introduce conflict 2 as follows:

    Serena is in the hallway by her locker. Mia walks up to her to talk about the rumors Serena has been spreading. How does Mia approach Serena? What does Mia say to Serena? Remember the SAFE communication skills. Mia and Serena aren't "dating partners," but this is an example of another relationship or conflict when the SAFE communication skills may be helpful.

11. After a few minutes, have the students switch roles again.

🗐 **Handout 27A**
🗐 **Handout 27B**

12. Pass out handout 27A, Conflict Situation 3, role-play descriptions and handout 27B, Conflict Skills Checklist 3, recorder's sheet.

13. Ask students to read the descriptions silently.

14. Introduce conflict 3 as follows:

    Jammal knocked on the door at Amara's house. Amara answers the door. She's surprised but happy to see him. Jammal is upset. What does he say to her?

PART 4
8 minutes

▶ **What If It Doesn't Work?**

The purpose of part 4 is to help students develop plans for when someone isn't communicating in a fair and open way.

1. Explain:

   Unfortunately, for communication skills to work and to produce a result that *both* people are happy with, both people have to cooperate. So what can you do when your girlfriend or boyfriend isn't doing her or his part?

2. Explain:

   I'm going to describe some conflicts in which one of the people is fighting fair, but the other person won't cooperate. After each description, I'm going to ask you

to develop back-up plans for the fair fighter so he or she can avoid getting frustrated and can avoid being physically or emotionally abused or abusive.

3. Read the following scenario out loud:

Chang and Lucy are arguing because they were supposed to meet at 6:00 P.M. but Lucy didn't show up until 7:00 P.M. She's been trying to explain why she was late and apologize, but Chang keeps interrupting her and insulting her for always being late, being rude, and so on. Lucy can't get anywhere.

4. Ask:

What can Lucy do if Chang is clearly not going to cooperate?

(Possible answers: tell him she'll talk to him later when he calms down; ask him directly and respectfully to be quiet so she can explain what happened; write him a letter; break up with him)

5. Read the next scenario to the class:

Tyler and Rachel are on their way to the movies in Rachel's car. She's mad because she saw Tyler flirting with his ex-girlfriend. He tries to explain they were just talking and that he doesn't want to be with his ex-girlfriend. Rachel can't seem to understand what he's saying to her. She pulls into the parking lot of the theater and starts yelling and screaming at him. She has slapped Tyler in the face before and seems as if she's ready to do it again.

6. Ask:

What can Tyler do since he can't seem to make Rachel calm down?

(Possible answers: get out of the car; call his parents or friends to come pick him up; point out to Rachel that there isn't anything he can do if she doesn't believe him)

PART 5
2 minutes

▶ **Conclusion**

1. Explain:

   Good communication between dating partners can help keep the power in relationships equal and can prevent abuse from happening. In relationships that are already abusive, communication skills may not be enough to help the victim.

   When victims of abuse try to use these skills, their efforts may be blocked because the abuser doesn't want to give the other person any power. In these situations, it's important to seek help outside of the relationship.

2. *Optional:* Have students add all their session 8 handouts to their journals. Remind them to bring their journals to the next session (if you don't collect them).

SESSION 9

Preventing Dating Sexual Abuse

Description

Through taking a quiz, analysis of scenarios, and a discussion with peers, students learn about the issue of dating sexual abuse and how to prevent it from happening.

Learner Outcomes

By the end of this session, students will be able to

- understand that victims of dating sexual abuse are never to blame

- understand that rape is always unacceptable

- understand and interpret "no" cues correctly

- know how to protect themselves in a potential rape situation

- state their sexual boundaries clearly to their dating partner

- describe dating tips to decrease their chances of being a victim of sexual assault or an abusive partner

- identify date rape drugs

SESSION 9
AT A GLANCE

Total Time: 50 minutes

Part 1: (10 minutes)
Sexual Assault Facts

Part 2: (13 minutes)
Paying Attention
to Signs

Part 3: (12 minutes)
Interpreting Signs

Part 4: (12 minutes)
Precautions

Part 5: (3 minutes)
Conclusion

Materials Needed

- ☐ ground rules poster (from session 1)
- ☐ *optional:* student journals (if students didn't keep them)
- ☐ Sexual Assault Quiz **Handout 28**
- ☐ pens or pencils
- ☐ six large pieces of paper or poster board
- ☐ two markers
- ☐ Caitlin and Samir Scenario **Handout 29**
- ☐ Dating Tips cards **Handout 30**
- ☐ prize for the Dating Tip scavenger hunt
- ☐ Date Rape Drug Precautions **Handout 31**

Preparation Needed

1. Read this session's background information.

2. Post the ground rules, if they aren't still up.

3. Write the six questions about the Samir and Caitlin scenario (found on pages 137–138) on the six pieces of poster board (one question on each piece of poster board).

4. Print and photocopy handouts 28, 29, and 31 (one for each student)

5. Print and photocopy the Dating Tips cards (handout 30). Cut out each of the eight different Dating Tips cards. Each student will be getting one card.

   Each shape on the cards is associated with one dating tip. Students will be mingling around to fill in all eight dating tips on their card. Make sure you'll have equal numbers of each card for your class.

Background Information

Teenagers between the ages of fifteen and nineteen are, as a group, the most likely to get raped and to experience sexual assault. Acquaintances commit these assaults and rapes more often than strangers; 60 percent of all rapes are acquaintance rapes. This session discusses some of the factors that place teens at risk for being a victim or perpetrator of date rape, stereotypes and myths about sexual violence, and tips for preventing dating sexual abuse.

Duplicating this page is illegal. Do not copy this material without written permission from the publisher.

133

SESSION 9 OUTLINE

PART 1
10 minutes

▶ **Sexual Assault Facts**

The purpose of part 1 is to define sexual assault in general so students are aware of how many actions constitute sexual assault and dating sexual abuse, and the many ways people may use sexual force. The purpose is also to clarify misperceptions about sexual assault in our society.

1. Explain:

   Today, we're going to talk about preventing one particular type of abuse in dating relationships—dating sexual abuse. Dating sexual abuse takes many forms, including unwanted sexual contact like forced oral sex; forced kissing; and unwanted fondling, grabbing, and touching. Dating sexual abuse also includes threats of unwanted sexual contact, attempted rape, and rape. Forced sexual acts at any time under any circumstance are crimes. Sexual abuse and rape by a date are as much of a crime as sexual abuse by a stranger.

   Sexual activity can be forced on someone in many different ways, from verbal persuasion, guilt, and emotional teasing to persistent attempts, threats, and physical force. Dating sexual abuse is an act of violence. Dating sexual abuse is a way of using sex as a weapon to gain power.

2. Explain:

   Before we really begin to talk about dating sexual abuse, I'm going to give you a short quiz about sexual assault in general. After you complete it, we'll talk about the answers.

 Handout 28

3. Hand out the Sexual Assault Quiz (handout 28) and give students five minutes to work through it.

4. Ask students to correct their own quiz. Discuss each answer to the quiz using the text below:

1. Sexual assault usually occurs because people cannot control their wild and spontaneous passions.

    False. *Sexual assault is an act of violence, not sex.*

2. Most people who commit rape appear to be well adjusted. They may even be well-liked and popular people.

    True. *Often the image of rapists that we have in our society is of crazed, mentally ill, obviously violent men. In reality, however, rapists may appear normal.*

3. One out of every four girls and one out of every six boys are sexually assaulted before they reach adulthood.

    True.

4. The majority of rapes occur between people of different races.

    False. *Most rapes occur between two people of the same race.*

5. The majority of rapes that are reported are committed by acquaintances, friends, or dates.

    True. *The FBI estimates that 60 percent of all reported rapes are acquaintance rapes.*

6. Date rape and acquaintance rape victims are most often teenagers.

    True. *Date and acquaintance rape victims are most often between the ages of fifteen and nineteen.*

7. If a girl gets a guy sexually excited, then it isn't rape if he forces her to have sex.

    False. *Rape is a forced act of sex no matter what the circumstances.*

8. Forced sexual activity isn't a crime if two people have been dating a long time and have had sex many times before.

   False. Sexual assault is any forced sexual activity no matter what the circumstances, and sexual assault is a crime.

9. Girls who try to resist rape are likely to get injured badly.

   False. Women who resist are the most likely to get away and the least likely to get injured. Seventy-five to 80 percent of women who immediately and actively resist sexual assault attempts avoid being raped. Sometimes girls do not yell or scream when they are being raped by a date because they are afraid of being embarrassed or of getting the boy into trouble. If someone is trying to rape you, try to leave the situation immediately, ask someone for help, or scream.

5. Explain:

   As you can see, many of the statements in this quiz are beliefs that many people hold but which aren't true. It's important for you to know the facts about sexual assault.

<table>
<tr><td>

PART 2

13 minutes

</td><td>

▶ **Paying Attention to Signs**

The purpose of part 2 is to point out the importance of paying attention to signs that dating partners are not ready to have sex.

1. Explain:

   The purpose of this next activity is to point out the importance of paying attention to signs that dating partners are not ready to have sex.

</td></tr>
</table>

🖴 Handout 29

2. Give the students a copy of handout 29, Caitlin and Samir Scenario.

3. Explain:

   I'm going to read you a scenario and then I am going to ask you some questions about it.

4. Read the Caitlin and Samir scenario.

5. Say:

   In this story, Samir raped Caitlin. Sexual activity can be forced on someone in many different ways, from verbal persuasion, guilt, and emotional teasing to frequent attempts, threats, and physical force. No matter what methods are used, if someone is forced to have sex without permission, it is rape and rape is a crime.

6. Ask the class the following questions and write the answers on the pieces of prepared poster board.

   a. **What did Samir do to force Caitlin to have sex?**

      (Possible answers: Samir insulted her and made her feel embarrassed for wanting to stop; he suggested that her wanting to stop was a sign that he was not important to her; he made her feel afraid; he told her he would take care of her; he made her think she would lose him if she did not have sex with him. No matter what methods are used, sex without permission is rape.)

   b. **Caitlin gave Samir signs that she did not want to have sex. What were the signs that Caitlin did not want to have sex?**

      (Possible answers: she told him to stop what he was doing several times; she said that she was scared; she started to cry and seemed unsure; she froze. Teens need to pay attention to the signs that their dates are not ready to have sex.)

   c. **Rape often causes serious physical and psychological problems. What are some bad things that could happen to Caitlin because of being raped?**

Duplicating this page is illegal. Do not copy this material without written permission from the publisher.

137

(Possible answers: Caitlin could become pregnant or get a sexually transmitted infection; she could have sexual and intimacy problems in the future; she could become depressed, anxious, and fearful; she may start having problems at school, at work, and with other activities that were once important to her before she was raped.)

d. What are some bad things that could happen to Samir because he raped Caitlin?

(Possible answers: Samir could be arrested and found guilty of rape; he could have a felony record for the rest of his life, which could prevent him from going to college or having a military career; he could get a sexually transmitted infection and father a child before he is ready; Samir could feel shame and guilt; Caitlin will likely stop dating him; word could get out that he has committed rape; he may have trouble in other relationships.)

e. What role could alcohol have played in this situation?

(Possible answer: drinking alcohol may cause people to do things they'll later regret.)

f. Are there places in the story where Samir could have done something different so that the story was less likely to end in rape?

(Possible answers: Samir should not have invited Caitlin to his house when his parents were not at home; they should not have been drinking beer; Samir made the mistake of taking Caitlin's coming to his house when his parents were not there as a sign that she wanted to have sex; he made the mistake of believing that Caitlin had had sex with her previous boyfriend based on the bragging of the boyfriend; even if Caitlin did have sex with her previous boyfriend, it would be a mistake for Samir to believe that she was ready to have sex with him; Samir ignored signs that Caitlin did not want to have sex; when Caitlin asked Samir to stop what he was doing and she said that she was scared, Samir should have immediately stopped trying to have sex with her.)

7. Explain:

This was date rape. It's important to recognize that forced sex at any time, under any circumstances, is rape and rape is a crime. Rape results in bad consequences for the victim and the person who commits the crime. The person who is forced to have sex is often blamed for it. However, it never is the fault of the person forced to have sex. There are no circumstances that make forced sexual acts okay. Samir could have prevented this from happening.

PART 3
12 minutes

▶ **Interpreting Signs**

The purpose of part 3 is to highlight the fact that males and females often aren't sending clear messages to one another. This confusion encourages people to rely on stereotypes to understand what's happening. It also sets up a scene for sexual assault.

1. Explain:

One of the reasons that rape may occur is that people on dates misinterpret cues or simply ignore them. Maybe Samir didn't recognize the signs that Caitlin wasn't ready to have sex. Maybe he thought her resistance meant something else. Many times boyfriends and girlfriends don't read signs from their partners in the way they were meant. As a result, misunderstandings arise.

2. Explain:

Now, I'm going to read you a few statements. I'd like the boys to respond to the statement first. Then I want the girls to respond to the statement. Then, we will compare and see when girls and boys agree and when they disagree.

3. Read the following statements to students. After each statement, allow time for a few boys to respond first and then a few girls.

a. When a girl dresses in tight, sexy clothing for a date, it means she definitely wants to have sex.

b. When a girl has had sex with other guys in the past, her boyfriend has the right to expect that she'll have sex with him.

c. When a girl freezes or is very still when a guy tries to have sex with her, it means she wants to have sex and the things he's doing are okay.

d. Girls resist sometimes just because they think that's what their boyfriends expect. Resisting really means they want to "go further."

e. When a girl goes into a bedroom with a boy while they're at a party, it means she wants to have sex with him.

f. Boys always want to have sex so they can't really be sexually assaulted or raped.

4. Ask:

What differences did you notice between the boys' responses and the girls' responses?

5. Ask:

What effect would these differences have on a date?

PART 4
12 minutes

▶ **Precautions**

The purpose of part 4 is to outline some ways to decrease the likelihood of being a victim or a perpetrator of sexual assault. Typically the focus is on how potential victims should change their behavior. This approach sometimes sounds as if it's the victim's responsibility to protect herself or himself, rather than the perpetrator's responsibility to change. This activity focuses on changes to be made by both potential victims and perpetrators. Remember, sexual assault is *never* the victim's fault.

1. Explain:

   Although all kinds of people are assaulted sexually in all kinds of places, there are some actions you can take to decrease the chance that you'll be seen as vulnerable, and therefore a potential victim. In addition, there are things that you can do to respect your partner's feelings and avoid violating her or his sexual boundaries.

2. Give the students the following instructions:

   The next exercise is a type of scavenger hunt. I'm going to pass out a card to each person. There is a different *Safe Dates* Dating Tip on each card next to a geometric shape. Don't show anyone your card until I say "Go."

   When I say "Go," get up and try to find all of the different dating tips in the room to fill in your Dating Tips card. There are eight different tips. Write each tip next to the matching shape on your card. The first person to show me a completed Dating Tips card gets a (describe the prize).

3. Pass out the previously prepared Dating Tips cards (handout 30) and pens or pencils (if needed). Then say, "Go."

4. After someone has gathered all of the dating tips, ask the students to return to their seats.

5. Ask the winner to read all of the tips. Have the other students complete their cards.

6. Explain:

   There's no way to guarantee that you won't be sexually assaulted, whether you're male or female. However, by listening to your feelings and using a few dating tips, you can reduce the chances that you'll be a victim.

   Discuss the dating tips on the next page.

Teacher's Tip ✓

Offer an inexpensive prize that will motivate teens to win (such as an unusual pen or a gift card for purchasing music).

 Handout 30

The Eight Dating Tips

Things I can do to protect myself:

1. Double-date or go out with groups of friends (on the first several dates).

2. Decide what your boundaries are about being sexual. Be clear and firm about your boundaries.

3. Trust your feelings and instincts. If you're uncomfortable, leave the situation and go to a safe place.

4. Be careful if your date holds strong gender stereotypes.

Things I can do to respect my partner:

1. Respect my date's feelings and wishes about being sexual.

2. Pay attention to my date's body language.

3. Be aware of my own gender stereotypes.

4. Stop my physical advances if my date says "no" or is unsure.

7. Explain:

It is also important for you to know that dating sexual abuse and rape drugs are becoming more common among teens. These drugs can be slipped into a drink so that date rape is easier. These drugs cause varying amounts of loss of consciousness.

Rohypnol (also called roofies, ruffies, roche [ro-shay], roach, R-2, and rope) is a very common type of date rape drug, but some other types are GHB, Ketamine, and Ecstasy. Some Rohypnol pills are small, round, and white. Newer Rohypnol pills are oval and green-gray in color. When slipped into a drink, a dye in these new pills makes clear liquids turn bright blue and dark drinks turn cloudy. But this color change might be hard to see in a dark drink, like cola or dark beer, or in a dark room. Also, pills with no dye are still available, making them impossible to see in a drink.

Also remember that alcohol is probably the most common dating sexual abuse and rape drug. More rapes have happened under the influence of alcohol than under the influence of any of the other drugs mentioned.

Handout 31

8. Give each student a copy of handout 31, Date Rape Drug Precautions, and go over the following precautions:

Date Rape Drug Precautions

- Don't put a drink down and leave it.

- Don't accept drinks from anyone you don't know well.

- Remember that dating sexual abuse and date rape is committed by people you know, so it is best to accept drinks that have not already been opened.

- Be especially careful about drinks at parties and clubs.

- Don't drink anything that tastes funny, even if your friends are drinking it.

- Don't drink alcohol. The majority of date rapes happen when someone has been drinking.

PART 5
3 minutes

▶ **Conclusion**

1. Summarize the session by discussing the following:

   Dating sexual abuse and rape are *never* the victim's fault. Be sure to pay attention to signs that your dating partner gives out, and be sure that you communicate your comfort level regarding sexual activity to your dating partner. Most importantly, listen to your partner, and make sure that your partner listens to you.

2. *Optional:* Have students add all their handouts from session 9 to their journals. Remind them to bring their journals to the next session (if you don't collect them).

Duplicating this page is illegal. Do not copy this material without written permission from the publisher.

143

SESSION 10

Reviewing the *Safe Dates* Program

Description

Through discussion, evaluation, and a poster contest, students will review the *Safe Dates* program.

Learner Outcomes

By the end of this session, students will be able to

- retain what they learned while participating in *Safe Dates*

**SESSION 10
AT A GLANCE**

Total Time: 50 minutes

Part 1: Optional
(20 minutes)
   Administering the
   Post-Test

Part 2: (20 minutes)
   Reviewing the *Safe
   Dates* program

Part 3: (8 minutes)
   Describe the
   Safe Dates
   Poster Contest

Part 4: (2 minutes)
   Conclusion

Materials Needed

- ☐ *optional:* post-test exam
- ☐ poster contest flyer
- ☐ prizes for poster contest winners
- ☐ *optional:* poster board or construction paper and art supplies for creating posters

Preparation Needed

1. *Optional:* Print and photocopy the post-test (one per student).
2. Create and photocopy a poster contest flyer (one per student). See the CD-ROM for an example.
3. Purchase prizes for the winners of the poster contest.
4. Set out art supplies for creating posters, if needed.

Background Information

A thorough review of the *Safe Dates* program will help students to retain and internalize what they have learned.

S E S S I O N **O U T L I N E**

PART 1
20 minutes

OPTIONAL

▶ **Administering the Post-Test**

The post-test is not a required part of the *Safe Dates* program, but because *Safe Dates* is often delivered in school settings where teachers want or need to assess student learning, a post-test is included on the CD-ROM. If you choose to deliver the post-test, it is suggested that it be administered before reviewing the program in part 2 of this session, as most of the answers to the questionnaire will be discussed during the review.

If the test was given prior to beginning *Safe Dates* as a pre-test, the answers can be compared to this post-test administration to assess changes in students' knowledge and attitudes. Or it can be given only after being exposed to *Safe Dates* and graded. Allow approximately twenty minutes to administer the post-test. If a more formal evaluation of *Safe Dates* is required, the *Safe Dates* Evaluation Questionnaire can be used in place of the post-test.

PART 2
20 minutes

▶ **Reviewing the *Safe Dates* Program**

1. Explain:

   This is our last session of the *Safe Dates* program and I'd like to take some time to review what we've learned.

2. Spend a few minutes reviewing some of the key concepts of the *Safe Dates* program. You may want to ask students to tell you what they learned. To guide this discussion, ask students some of the following questions:

   a. **What are some things you'd look for in a caring dating relationship?**

   b. **What are some examples of physical dating abuse? Emotional dating abuse?**

   c. **Why do people abuse in dating relationships?**

d. What are some of the key steps to helping a friend in an abusive dating relationship?

e. How do gender stereotypes affect dating relationships?

f. What are some positive ways to handle anger in relationships?

g. What are the four SAFE skills for effective communication in dating relationships?

h. What are some ways to protect yourself from being a victim of dating sexual abuse?

i. What are things you can do to prevent yourself from using dating sexual abuse?

3. Review with students where they can go for help if they or their friends are victims or perpetrators of dating abuse. Review both school and local community resources.

PART 3
8 minutes

▶ **Describe the *Safe Dates* Poster Contest**

Hosting a poster contest is a great way to reinforce the concepts learned in this curriculum. The poster contest is an activity that's best done after completing the curriculum. Posters on the theme of dating abuse prevention can be displayed in school hallways or other community buildings such as libraries, city hall, and shopping malls. Students could also use their posters in presentations to various school or community groups. A key aspect of the poster contest is that the posters are displayed in locations where other students taking the *Safe Dates* program can see them. Having students in the class or school vote on the best posters is a good way to ensure that students are exposed to the messages in the posters. Prizes can be offered for first, second, and third place. The sample poster contest flyer on the CD-ROM can be changed to accommodate the type of contest your school or agency desires. For example, instead of creating posters, students could develop media messages, Web sites, or text messages, as long as students taking *Safe Dates* have an opportunity to view or hear the messages created.

1. Hand out the poster contest flyer you have created. Read through this flyer together so students know the guidelines for the contest.

2. If there's time, allow students to begin creating their posters. After this session, students will work on the posters on their own time.

PART 4
2 minutes

▶ **Conclusion**

1. Congratulate all students for the hard work they put into learning the *Safe Dates* program.

2. *Optional:* Allow students to keep their journals. Encourage them to review the material in their journals regularly. It will remind them of the key things they should do to prevent dating abuse.

Hazelden, a national nonprofit organization founded in 1949, helps people reclaim their lives from the disease of addiction. Built on decades of knowledge and experience, Hazelden offers a comprehensive approach to addiction that addresses the full range of patient, family, and professional needs, including treatment and continuing care for youth and adults, research, higher learning, public education and advocacy, and publishing.

A life of recovery is lived "one day at a time." Hazelden publications, both educational and inspirational, support and strengthen lifelong recovery. In 1954, Hazelden published *Twenty-Four Hours a Day,* the first daily meditation book for recovering alcoholics, and Hazelden continues to publish works to inspire and guide individuals in treatment and recovery, and their loved ones. Professionals who work to prevent and treat addiction also turn to Hazelden for evidence-based curricula, informational materials, and videos for use in schools, treatment programs, and correctional programs.

Through published works, Hazelden extends the reach of hope, encouragement, help, and support to individuals, families, and communities affected by addiction and related issues.

For questions about Hazelden publications, please call 800-328-9000

or visit us online at hazelden.org/bookstore.